D1563437

Ethical Choices in
Contemporary Medicine

Also by Raphael Sassower and published by McGill-Queen's University Press

Popper's Legacy: Rethinking Politics, Economics and Science

Ethical Choices in Contemporary Medicine
Integrative Bioethics

Raphael Sassower and Mary Ann Cutter

McGill-Queen's University Press
Montreal & Kingston · Ithaca

© Raphael Sassower and Mary Ann Cutter, 2007

ISBN 978-0-7735-3350-9 (hardcover)
ISBN 978-0-7735-3351-6 (paperback)

Legal deposit fourth quarter 2007
Bibliothèque nationale du Québec

Published simultaneously in the United Kingdom by Acumen
Publishing Limited and in North America by McGill-Queen's University
Press

Library and Archives Canada Cataloguing in Publication

Sassower, Raphael
  Ethical choices for contemporary medicine : integrative
bioethics / Raphael Sassower and Mary Ann Cutter.

Includes bibliographical references and index.
ISBN 978-0-7735-3350-9 (bound)
ISBN 978-0-7735-3351-6 (pbk.)

  1. Medical ethics—Philosophy.   2. Bioethics—Philosophy.
I. Cutter, Mary Ann Gardell.   II. Title.

R724.S27 2007   174.2   C2007-904929-X

Typeset by Graphicraft Limited, Hong Kong.
Printed and bound by Cromwell Press, Trowbridge.

Contents

Introduction

Our primary goal is to argue in favour of "integrative bioethics".
Integrative bioethics embeds bioethical reflection in a confluence
of disciplines that provide an appreciation of different aspects
of medical practice and bring into view different concerns and
possible pathways for intervening to address health care needs.
The problem is this: medicine is usually viewed as a rigorous, fact-
based science that provides certain knowledge in matters related
to health and disease. On the basis of such a view, the core activities of medicine (e.g. diagnosis, treatment and prognosis) are not
open to public scrutiny and debate in the same way other social
activities might be. Medical disputes are then resolved as if they
were matters of fact, rather than as sociopolitical matters subject
to ethical and philosophical reflection that optimally lead to an
open-minded dialogue. Complementing this reductionist view of
medicine is the traditional principle-based ethic, which sees value
disputes as independent of the complex network of relations that
characterize medical practice. According to this view, individuals
can appeal to specific principles to justify their claims or choices.
The principle approach in bioethics and the specific expression of

the rights-based approach are examples of this reductionist view of medicine.

As an alternative to this view of medicine and its attendant view of bioethics, we advocate an "integrative bioethics" that involves a deeper appreciation of how questions of facts and values, and knowing and doing, are intertwined within particular contexts. Integrative bioethics will involve a confluence of or collaboration among different disciplines that help to provide an appreciation of multiple aspects of medical practice, and possible avenues for responding to health care needs. In practice, there is a feedback loop that can keep us much better informed of what we might neglect to account for. In some cases, a clinical decision-making process could benefit from the experiences of other patients, even though each patient's conditions are unique. Likewise, medical knowledge claims are significant starting points for treatment, but must be supplemented by personal histories (to ascertain genetic propensities for contracting certain viruses) and the environmental circumstances within which patients are diagnosed (abject poverty or obesity may bring about or exacerbate a medical condition).

What we promote in this book is an alliance among health care providers and among patients, past, present and future, so that we all appreciate the extent to which we can help each other discover ways of alleviating pain and suffering and recognize the obstacles that lay ahead of us, whether technical in nature or cognitive. In no way do we relinquish our hope in or minimize the great strides undertaken by the more scientific side of medicine. Instead, we would like to enjoy these strides in more meaningful ways when we couch them in broader cultural frameworks, where traditional therapies and remedies have had an enormous effect on people's health. Lest we are misunderstood, we should hasten to add that our concern is not to replace traditional allopathic medicine with alternative or holistic medicine, but to complement it with a level of self-reflection that could shed light on some of the most obvious ways in which we learn from our practices and improve our health conditions. One's health is not limited to the maintenance of one's organs, but also includes and incorporates information about the kind of diet one enjoys, the environment in which one lives, and the people with whom one interacts. As the ancients taught us, our health includes our physical, psychological, emotional and intellectual well-being, and only with a balance among all these components can we hope to promote and preserve it. Given that we are both philosophers by training, we appeal to the Socratic insistence that the unexamined life is not worth living.

Our strategy in this book is to highlight some of the issues faced by patients and health care professionals in contemporary culture as a way to revisit the historical and philosophical debates that have perennially been cross-cultural. Concerns with the efficacy of scientific knowledge in general and some drugs and procedures in particular are symptomatic of deeper and more substantial concerns over scientific and therefore medical epistemology. There are concerns about how medical knowledge is established (scientific validity) and how medical protocols are administered (checks and balances), how medical certainty is evaluated (probability) and medical responsibility is framed (personal or collective), and how medical knowledge is transmitted (popular media versus professional journals) and medical care is allocated (insurance policies and government subsidies).

In general, this book addresses the present predicaments of medicine, such as the status of medical knowledge and medical certainty, within a broad cultural context that exposes the expectations individuals have of their health care providers, of health care institutions and of themselves. We explore some of the historical roots of these concerns and suggest that rational discourse – that is, a constricted way to use reason to explore alternative answers to pressing questions – and parochial ethical dialogue – that is, a method restricted to a set of particular beliefs – may be futile in the face of competing and incommensurable frameworks and agendas, attitudes and wishes. Instead of focusing on public debates and highlighting the respective perspectives from which the protagonists frame their positions, we are reaching to the broader epistemological issues that might offer more useful insights and answers to the questions that are raised at the public debates level. What we mean by epistemology in this context is the accumulation of knowledge in the broadest sense of the term that may be assumed or forgotten, but that can be identified or recognized once certain practices are challenged.

For example, when the media sensationalizes "cloning", whether of animals or humans, what is missing from the discussion is the kind of integrative analysis we recommend. Some argue the scientific basis for such a procedure and get mired in the debates of the potential for a one-to-one matching of one's genes. Others jump into the fray and argue about human dignity and the violation – ethical, social, political and otherwise – of the duplication of humans and the potential abuses of such a technique. What is missing from either extreme of the spectrum of dialogues is the deeper appreciation of what the biological basis is, and also what issues may be moot because of that basis. Surely, the biological basis (what can and cannot be done in principle, let alone in laboratory practice) is itself being contested, so that the so-called parochial debate may be misguided. In short, one needs to consider as much as possible of the epistemological input simultaneously in order to get a glimpse of what is reasonable to argue about. Otherwise, we expend a great deal of energy just to recast our presuppositions and deflect potential criticism and thus render the debate futile.

Lest we forget, the art of medicine has as much to do with useful medical practice and its scientific bases, and so it allows for greater variation in treatment and comes short of having definitive answers to medical questions. For example, as we detail later on, the approach to cancer is fraught with scientific controversy (What are the origins? How does it spread? Can it be genetically isolated?) so that any evaluation of treatment is bound to be complex and lead to disagreements about efficacy. In order to anchor our theoretical concerns, we provide a rich set of discussions drawn from the history of philosophy, medicine, science and technology as useful examples that lead up to the present situation in the western world. It is in this sense, then, that this is not a social science tract that attempts to couch all epistemological and ethical discussions within a social context or reduce them to social relations. The perennial debate over the "art", "technology" and "science" of medicine and the apprenticeship standards applied for centuries is only one of many that illustrate how we tend to overlook the major predicament of its practitioners. When we say this, we mean to focus on the challenges that face practitioners in terms of what assumptions are being used in their practices rather than in what particular power relations they find themselves.

We emphasize that, in the postmodern age (by which we simply mean at this stage an age that attempts to surpass the limitations of the modern age where a set of principles and beliefs were assumed to guide all decision-making processes), two interrelated issues surface when it comes to medicine. On the one hand, there is a strong critique of science and the privileges associated with the scientific discourse and, on the other, there is still a deep-seated quest for certainty in all medical matters (e.g. Do *I* have cancer? Can it be cured *now*? What precisely is *my* prognosis?). The critique of science in general finds a particularly painful outlet in the case of medicine, where pharmaceuticals are constantly attacked yet remain the "holy grail" for technological advances and the saviours of human life. When we recall how precarious the scientific or empirical status of medicine is to begin with, then it would come as no surprise that statistical data and probabilistic responses to patient enquiries remain obscure and frustrating: they cannot get a straight answer! What we mean in this area is that knowledge claims are not certain because they are historically and ideologically bound: they are limited by what is known at the time, and that knowledge, as we have seen, is a moving target.

Finally, it is with all of these concerns in mind that we have come to appreciate the deep and everlasting ethical dimensions that continue to appear at every juncture of medical discourse, from research to production, from distribution to consumption. Our main contribution here is to replace the standard "medical ethics" models of "autonomy" or "rights" language with a more comprehensive appreciation of epistemological frameworks and the ethical commitments they implicitly contain. This appreciation is based on the procedures by which we must contextualize what we say or do about diseases and the suffering of patients. To say that we integrate a variety of approaches and viewpoints means that we encourage practitioners to consult alternative diagnoses, therapies and prognoses to those with which they are familiar.

There are a few premises that underlie this book and that need to be disclosed at the outset. To begin with, there needs to be a greater shift from medical ethics and the debates surrounding its current prominence in the academy and in medical institutions, like hospitals and research centres, to the philosophy of medicine. Here philosophy of medicine is understood not as a defined discipline, but as a process by and through which reflections on clinical knowledge and practice and medical research and public policy meet to produce insights and suggestions regarding how health and disease are understood and manipulated. For us, there is much more fruitful potential in the critical examination of the historical, sociological, economic and moral aspects and manifestation of medical practices – what some may simply see as being philosophically minded – than in the limited discussions related to the rights of physicians and patients or the conflicts that arise when these rights clash in particular settings. Our recommendation to open lines of communication is not supposed to be yet another "approach" that jettisons all other approaches or that is superior to them in any way; instead, it is an invitation to be more inclusive and curious of alternative ways of examining how our health and well-being are understood and treated and should be differently studied. There is much more fruitful discussion in an integrative approach to bioethics than the emerging single-disciplinary approach evident in contemporary medicine, as we explore later.

The second premise has to do with the "fact" that medicine has always been and will always remain an art as well as a science. As an art, it is a practice that requires apprenticeship and not simply a modern academic mastery of scientific data. As an art, it is also an individualistic or subjective endeavour that requires sensitivity to personal circumstances and the conditions of treatment, so that broad models and empirical data remain guidelines applicable in some but not all cases. As a science, it is an endeavour that has built-in uncertainties that no research of a collection of data can ever overcome. As a science, it is also an undertaking that depends on technological breakthroughs and instruments, so that it becomes technoscience in the deepest sense of the term. If we add the two components of medicine (art and science), we find that the theoretical and practical are intertwined and continue to inform each other as they go along. No theoretical framework about infection and immunology, for example, can ever provide full-proof protocols for treatment. Anecdotal evidence from diverse populations, at times, can be as informative as laboratory research on rats.

The third premise of this book has to do with our belief that philosophical ideas and frameworks influence the culture in which we live. In turn, cultural ideas influence individual views, opinions and expectations. This means that in order to understand our personal frustrations or hopes, we must study the history of ideas and the particular ways in which it has brought us into this century. It also means that we must make explicit our implicit assumptions about the role of society in protecting and enhancing the well-being of the individual. For example, any discussion of the ethics of prolonging or ending life in the clinical setting (active or passive euthanasia) must be understood against the backdrop of the extent to which medicine in the early twenty-first century has been able to understand the biology of life and death (the functioning of our physiology at any level, cellular, organic or genetic). As the saying goes, we do it because we can. Our medical capacities to intervene in life and death are not immune from the economic and religious influences of a culture (with its traditions and beliefs), which will find support or criticism of what medicine can do. The point here is that reflection upon what we do in medicine and what we think we must do is nested within a greater cultural context that deserves recognition if we are going to understand why certain debates rage (assisted suicide, for example) and others remain relatively quiet (proper diet, or assistance to the poor, for example).

Fourthly, we believe that personal expectations about health care must be framed within the confines of reason. By this we mean that we cannot expect too much out of a system of health care provision that has inherent limitations, both technoscientific and financial. This means that though we could have "perfect" health care whatever it may mean personally, we could not afford to have such care for everyone all the time. There are constraints and limits to what we can rationally provide throughout the world without exhausting all our resources, whether we live within a socialist or capitalist system. Depleting these resources would undermine and hurt many other aspects of our lives that indirectly contribute to living a healthy life, such as public safety and living wages for those who are in the workforce. Obviously, the presumption here is that we have scarce rather than abundant resources with which to deal with human needs and desires. Here, too, the issue is not what can ideally be accomplished with our medical knowledge, but what choices are routinely made based on the availability of resources. This is why public policy is important as a starting point for philosophical and personal reflection. Who are we? What do we value? What priorities have we made? Should they be changed?

The fifth premise has to do with the recognition of the incredible privilege we have in developed countries considering our entitlement to health care. This premise has to do with the incredible wealth we assume to be the basis of our freedoms and rights, and our sense of entitlement as citizens, which is expressed in national constitutions regarding the right to life. We take it for granted that infant mortality should be zero and that life expectancy should continue to rise indefinitely. There is a hidden expectation that death is a nuisance that can be avoided with enough ingenuity and will, as if immortality is a reasonable goal to be achieved within the present century. In some perverse sense, our great fortunes have led us to certain sets of ethical quandaries that others, in less fortunate positions, cannot even consider because they are worried about much more basic freedoms and rights related to survival. For example, when is the price of prolonging life for two weeks of an eighty-nine-year-old too much? When is the price of saving an infant with multiple abnormalities who may die in three months too high, if ever? Has medical prowess been so seductive that we have all succumbed to its lure without self-criticism or self-reflection?

These premises inform our appreciation of the predicaments of medical practices – What should we do? How should we explain what we do? Who should we be accountable to? – as they unfold in individual cases and in the popular media. The predicaments can be outlined in the following ways. First, patients want to know more about medicine and health than ever before, but are often intimidated by the technical jargon that accompanies anything medical (the use of Latin terms and short-hand classification of disease). Secondly, clinicians know the limits of their knowledge and those of their treatments, but may feel compelled to offer more than they can deliver because of their patients' expectations (the patient is a consumer who demands answers and expects results). Thirdly, the public expects that health care providers will cure all their illnesses without realizing that such expectation is untenable (the syndrome of the "the sky is the limit"). Fourthly, the public expects that, in order to receive optimal health care, no personal sacrifices would be required (one pill will cure all the problems without requiring any lifestyle changes, such as diet, exercise or work habits). And, fifthly, there is a sense of entitlement (we deserve perfect health care provision) that is not accompanied by a sense of responsibility (we have the duty to take care of ourselves, in terms of diet, lifestyle, risk-taking and the like, as well as to be willing to pay more taxes in order to achieve our goals).

In some sense, the conclusions that we advocate are not new. There have been a host of others (notably physicians Edmund Pellegrino, H. Tristram Engelhardt Jr and Henrik Wulff) who have argued that bioethics needs to be embedded in the broad reflections of the philosophy of medicine, as we understand it to mean being philosophically minded and integrating variety of approaches and methods of inquiry. Many of these same advocates have argued extensively for understanding the value-laden character of facts and the historicity of medical knowledge. One such advocate is Paul Starr, for example, who has woven a rich analysis of historical and sociological data from the American context. What concerns us is that these voices are often isolated in the literature to a shift to the social sciences (e.g. Starr's (1982) narrative of the transformation of medical practice in the USA), a discussion of concepts of disease (e.g. Engelhardt's (1981) treatment of the disease of masturbation) or an examination of the value of the patient–physician relationship (e.g. Pellegrino 1976). Their suggestions – that any thoughtful resolution cannot take place without broad considerations of the assumptions, history and broader context of the conflict within medicine – are often lost in the bioethical case study analysis literature.

Although some may find our approach to be an elaboration on their work, and some may wish our work to be more inclusive of every variant that has appeared in every subdiscipline, we think that our work does offer something novel: our method itself is an expression of how to achieve our prescribed goals of an integrative bioethics. On some level, we exemplify what we prescribe: we draw from various sources, we provide a broad context for discussion and we refrain from being single-minded advocates for this or that method of inquiry (not all of medicine can be reduced into this or that idea or principle). It is not simply drawing from this or that source, nor simply showing that philosophy of medicine and philosophy of science (broadly construed) are linked to epistemology and ontology, and therefore will inform any ethical decision. Instead, we reframe the problems and the discussions in such a way that all of these sources and approaches come together within open-ended and multifactorial frameworks.

Obviously, the predicaments outlined here are only a selection of a wider range of challenges, but they help to illustrate what kind of personal anxiety is felt by patients in the twenty-first century. As philosophers by training and not physicians, we speak in generalities and not in detailed, clinical terms. This means that we do not begin our discussion with lengthy case studies that inform our views (as does Jerome Groopman 2007), and that then are weaved together to provide a quilt of revelation (e.g. doctors do not listen carefully to their patients, and therefore make more mistakes than they should). Nor are we social scientists who detect trends and fashions in health providers' behaviour and then draw conclusions about social relations and cultural socialization (e.g. Latour's (1988) analysis of the "Pasteurization of France"). Likewise, when we use historical anecdotes and cases, we use them to illustrate our views and concerns, rather than generalizing from them to the culture as a whole or providing a historiography of medical progress.

In this fashion, we remain philosophically minded and interested in integrative medicine so as to challenge current approaches in bioethics. To be clear, we use the term "integrative" to refer to the collaboration among different disciplines and perspectives from which medical practices can be perceived. The collaboration at times subsumes a variety of methods of inquiry and at times foregrounds some at the expense of others for pragmatic purposes. The value of this approach is to undermine the uniform direction in which bioethical discussion may be heading – that is, it is a way to open up a discussion that would be otherwise thwarted. But let us be clear, as well, about what the term "integrative medicine" means for others, who work with different goals in mind.

For some, like Zuzana Parusnikova (2002), the issue is whether or not medical practice could become more aligned with notions of partnership than with standard power relations whose legitimacy arises from their scientific and technological expertise or authority. Others, like Andrew Weil (2004), are concerned with health as partially, but significantly, influenced by the environmental conditions under which we lead our lives. For them, nutrition and lifestyle choices are just as relevant or complementary variables in maintaining one's health as any other western-style intervention and treatment. Still others, such as Deepak Chopra (2003), promote the spiritual dimensions of health and well-being, suggesting that whether the influence is eastern- or western-based, tranquility and transcendence are essential ingredients in the promotion of health and well-being. Finally, there are some, such as Christiane Northrup (1998), who focus on the healing potential of women in terms of their ability to transform their own conditions and become advocates of the healing powers inherent in their bodies. Although we do not subscribe to any of these approaches whole-heartedly, we find them all inspirational in the sense of enforcing our own suspicion that we must reject the single-minded and reductionistic biases of western-style medical care. Our approach is hereby aligned with theirs, but is more focused on bioethics. Herein lies the novelty of the proposals that follow.

We are conceptual geographers, so to speak, who map out the intellectual (epistemological) and ethical terrain and thereby uncover the reasons why certain developments have taken place. We use the compasses of the past in order to figure out the directions that were chosen, without thereby limiting the potential for shifting directions and making different choices in the future. In this sense, then, we hope to shed some light on how we came to be in the position in which we find ourselves today, and perhaps offer a critique that would encourage us to redirect our efforts when the need arises. The position we are in might be upsetting to those who would like a more rational method of health care provision as well as those who would like the bioethical debates about medical care to make more sense. But perhaps it is liberating to those who suspect that human knowing and acting take place within contexts that evolve and overlap, without absolute certainty or predictability.

,

1

The predicaments of contemporary medicine

The debate over the nature and definition of medicine is as old as our recorded western history. Eighteen hundred years ago, Galen defined medicine as an art (*techne*) and tried to distinguish between the empiricist and rationalist trends in the field. How much should experience (collected empirical data) influence the practice of medicine? Should reason (rational and logical deduction of effects from a set of causes) play an important role in the theoretical construction of a medical model? Depending on how these two questions are answered, we will have a better idea about how to train students of medicine. These questions have reappeared at the dawn of the twenty-first century because of our increased reliance on technoscience, the confluence and interwoven emergence of scientific theories and models and technological instruments and innovations.

This reliance, as we shall explain in the second section, is not limited to specific breakthroughs in biochemistry or genetics, but is pervasive in the atmosphere in which we come across public health issues. Questions about medicine as art and as science, as the third section will illustrate, are also tied to changing public expectations with regard to the promises of democracy and capitalism. And finally, the questions raised and answered here bring together a multidisciplinary or integrative approach to the widening field of medicine in the twenty-first century.

The art of medicine

In order to appreciate the extent to which medicine is both an art and technoscience, we should also note how medicine relates to biology. If, as Charles Coulston Gillispie reminds us, our conceptions of nature in general and biology in particular were not well articulated centuries ago, then it would make perfect sense that medicine as a field of practice would not have a strict definition or a strict set of parameters within which to operate. Here is Gillispie on biology:

> It is, indeed, indicative of the inchoate nature of these subjects that the word "biology" had to await the nineteenth century to be coined. In the sixteenth and seventeenth centuries the subjects it was to embrace scarcely had an independent existence. Anatomy and physiology were rather aspects of medicine than science, and medicine was oriented more toward art and therapy than knowledge. Although human anatomy was studied more by analogy to animals than from cadavers, this practice was the source rather of error than of comparative anatomy, which does not antedate the eighteenth century. Natural history, for its part, was pursued rather in the spirit of the bird-watcher or the moralist than the investigator.
>
> (Gillispie 1960: 58–9)

Medicine as we know it had developed over time to become more rather than less scientific in the senses advocated by the leaders of the scientific revolutions in Europe during the sixteenth and seventeenth centuries. G. E. R. Lloyd (1995) reminds us that, historically, medicine was considered imprecise and therefore a craft and an art whose practice was valued but whose predictive ability was questionable. As he quotes from Plato's *Phaedrus* (260e), "the proper practice of medicine as an art is contrasted with its practice merely as a knack and by experience". He also quotes the *Philebus* (55e ff.): "where the arts are graded according to their degree of exactness, medicine comes in the lowest category, along with music, farming, navigation and generalship, below carpentry, which makes more use of instruments designed to achieve exactness" (Bates 1995: 35). Whether medicine was considered art or science bothered our predecessors less, according to Luis Garcia-Ballester, than its usefulness. Speaking of the Latin west, he says that:

> The concept of usefulness (*utilitas*) was closely linked to the justification of the physician's presence in society, both among non-academic social groupings – by demonstrating the efficacy of his knowledge through practice – and in the academic community itself. The presence of physicians in the latter was justified only as long as they were able to train *artfices* (*phisici, cirurgici*) who might solve the problems of health arising in the community that the university served. (Bates 1995: 145)

Utility alone was not what marked medicine as worthy of study and practice. In accumulating medical knowledge, physicians learned how to diagnose diseases and how to treat them. But, as we shall see in Chapter 2, the focus on diseases and their characteristics is itself problematic. According to Andrew Wear (1995), with reference to the sixteenth century, "The learned physician's trademark was that he took into account the patient, and that it was the individual patient and not the disease that had to be treated, so that one remedy could not cure all who suffered from the same disease" (Bates 1995: 163).

Defining medicine as an art or technique rather than a science makes a difference in how we approach the discipline and the practice. We would not argue that medicine is only an art or that it lacks any scientific basis. Instead, we would suggest that the scientific basis of medicine provides only a provisional starting point for the practice of medicine, and that as such medicine is a techno-scientific practice (Delkeskamp-Hayes & Cutter 1993). This suggestion is encountered daily by those going to their health care provider, a doctor or nurse, a clinician or pharmacist, in order to be diagnosed or receive prescription. There are no clear-cut answers, no absolute certainty, but instead a carefully nuanced response regarding the patient's medical condition. Why can we not provide clear and simple answers? (More on this in Chapter 4.)

Incidentally, the recognition that medicine is more of an art than a science is most pronounced in the contemporary structure of medical education (Sassower 1990a), where the first two years of rigorous scientific training are followed by two years of rotation among all the subdisciplines of medical practice. Let us be clear here that when we talk about the art of medicine, we do not follow a social science approach that would enumerate case studies in which anecdotal evidence provides the only theoretical foundation, as, for example, Paul Starr (1982) does when describing the changing practices of health care provision in America. A theoretical judgement is being tested in practice, and the practice supports a theoretical conviction. So, what is the status of medical knowledge? Does it have the certitude expected of geometric calculations? Or is it open to the perennial Cartesian doubt (Descartes 1980) and ongoing revisions? If there is an inherent uncertainty concerning medical knowledge, then anything from medical diagnosis to prognosis becomes more nuanced and subtle than if it were wholly scientific. If physicians can only tell patients the probability of some set of variables leading to a particular disease and its treatment potential, then how can patients ever know their own specific fate? What meaning can we ascribe to probability values (Todhunter 1865)? How should they be understood, interpreted and calculated for individual cases (if such a thing is even possible)? What probabilistic answers should patients accept or doubt?

These are real questions that face real participants in the medical community on a daily basis, as was also documented by Bruno Latour in his documentation of the changing practices and attitudes in France in relation to Pasteur's discoveries (Latour 1988, especially Ch. 3). These are not esoteric concerns but the concerns of us all, because they undermine our belief in the clear-cut answers we expect of medicine as science, not realizing that science itself has been open to critical examination since the latter half of the twentieth century (Sassower 1995). The status of scientific claims has come under scrutiny because theoretical commitments change over time, and the basic assumptions that set the foundation of science remain open to multiple interpretations, if not to radical revisions. Concerns over knowledge claims in general and scientific claims in particular permeate the history of ideas, because much was at stake in making claims about nature without reference to divine revelation. Karl Popper's (1959) debates with the Vienna Circle in the early part of the twentieth century have only streamlined and raised greater urgency to these debates about the status of scientific knowledge itself. It was David Hume (1978) who in the modern era questioned the principle of induction, our ability logically to move from causes to effects, from a set of empirical data to a generalized conclusion. When Popper followed suit and proposed his principle of falsification, all he attempted to do was resurrect faith in scientific certainty. He likewise criticized some of his disciples and adversaries – Paul Feyerabend (1975) and Thomas Kuhn (1970) come to mind – with regard to their cavalier introduction of irrationalism into the scientific fold, which would ultimately undermine our faith in science.

We recite some of these anecdotes in the modern history of science so as to alert ourselves to the precarious status science itself has had to protect, so that when we speak of the scientific status of medicine we will be doubly cautious. Perhaps the view of medicine as art rather than science would fare better if the public learned to lower its expectations of its performance while still retaining the belief that medicine is a highly valued practice that can save lives (as Engel 1977 and Pellegrino 1976 have already done). We should hasten to add that public expectations of science and of medicine are poorly founded, for they rely on mass media for their highly sensational, inaccurate and (more often than not) positive appeal. High-drama, primetime television series, such as *ER*, contribute to the misinformation about the workings of medicine, because they focus on the personal lives of physicians and nurses and the drama of the hospital setting, leaving aside (assuming away) the contested scientific status of medicine itself.

As we continue to consider some of the influences on the conceptualization and practice of medicine, we would like to suggest that there is a great deal to be gained from the philosophical context under which medicine is scrutinized. If we limit our inquiry to the advantages and shortfalls in the application of medicine, we are already accepting a utilitarian framework (in which benefits are maximized in the light of pain or suffering; see Bentham 1970) without testing whether it is the appropriate or defensible one to be used here. It seems to us that the development and proliferation of the subdisciplines concerned with medical ethics have poorly served academics and the public with regard to medicine (Sassower & Grodin 1988). If all we focus on is rights or autonomy language in a hospital setting (the conflicting rights of patients, nurses, doctors and insurance companies), we miss too much to be able to make an intelligent choice. For example, the standard issues of the past thirty years revolved, among other things, around reproductive rights, the right to die and the dilemmas of health care delivery. In many cases, these issues were raised as if autonomous and well-informed individuals were in the position of making rational choices given a set of alternatives (Annas 1988). But has this been the case? Have these individuals not been part of a culture whose convictions and ideology (religious and moral) might be alienated from the (capitalist and individualistic) culture of hospitals and physicians? Have we assumed away some differences that would have provided radically different models for discussing alternative choices?

If we consider the question of death in cases of accidents or terminal diseases (rather than what we call natural death), is it reasonable (not to mention accurate) to call *organ*-sustaining machines *life*-supporting? The very question at hand – is the patient alive? – is being answered before the question is raised, because stopping the equipment is tantamount to killing the patient. But if the machines are only maintaining the function of certain organs, then we leave open the question of whether the patient is indeed being kept alive or has been dead before being hooked to the machines. It may seem a linguistic quibble to some, but in our view this is a crucial distinction that can circumvent, if not eliminate, some painful controversies regarding death (Sassower & Grodin 1986). Likewise, if we viewed the medical profession through a prism wider than that reserved for science proper, we would appreciate a certain fluidity and uncertainty that is inherent in the practice of medicine. Once again, it might seem relatively unimportant what scientific status we accord medicine on a theoretical or philosophical level, but we suggest that it would make all the difference in the world when it comes to disputes about therapies, expectations about the efficacy of treatment and the inevitable limitations of diagnoses and prognoses.

In this context, then, we wish to plead for a century in which philosophy of medicine takes centre-stage in deliberations concerning health care. Even when biochemical or genetic research is undertaken, we would like to know what assumptions are being used, what philosophical beliefs are being played out and what ideological convictions are being implicitly promoted. On this particular point, the work of Richard Lewontin (1993) is relevant, because he helps to expose the ideological underpinnings of debates in biology. To believe that we merely practise medicine or that we merely build on our medical experiences (as Galen already noted) is to refuse to admit that we have theoretical and ideological commitments that influence how we think and practise our trade. Our theoretical commitments are eventually made explicit, for instance, when we try to map the human genome with the belief that an individual gene causes a specific disease. But what if this turns out to be false, as appears to be the case, and only a certain combination of genes and other DNA matter is more or less likely to contribute to specific diseases? As Lander & Schrok (1994: 2037) convincingly argue, "most traits of medical relevance do not follow simple Mendelian monogenic inheritance". What they tease out in their survey of the literature and the experimental data is a rejection of a reductionist view of cause and effect (the ability to provide a direct and unitary correspondence between specific items) and instead the adoption of a more complex, evolutionary view of human physiology, genetics, medicine and the environment.

We would like to suggest in this book that medicine has never been nor will ever be an activity undertaken in isolation from the rest of the culture in which it is situated. The success or failure of medical practitioners depends on the support and expectations related to the field. The medical community operates with guidelines that include medical practices, economic considerations, institutional codes and moral obligations. It would, therefore, be misleading to examine medicine apart from its cultural settings and the pressures under which it must operate. For example, we have to examine what questions are being addressed by the medical profession and why these are the questions that are being raised to begin with. Should we address questions about preventive medicine rather than questions about the efficacy of triple bypass operations for overweight white males? What legitimates one set of questions over the other? Who is responsible for putting one set of questions on the research funding agenda of the National Institutes of Health? Does a "right to health care" make any sense without a sustained discussion of who has what responsibility to provide for the resources to satisfy such a right (e.g. kidney dialysis in 1976)? How is it that we have assumed that AIDS only affects gay males? How do we even begin to think about national responses to emerging infectious diseases and bioterrorism?

Examining the questions that make it to the citadels of the medical establishment can shed light on the presumptions used by funding agencies when research proposals flood the gates of these agencies. The disproportional funding of research into the diseases that are more common in white elderly males as opposed to women of colour illustrates our concern. Likewise, examining the culture of technoscience would shed light on certain prejudices we have with regard to the workings of science in general and medicine in particular. A mechanistic view of the world (a machine-like model wherein each part contributes to the functioning of the whole) would lead us to view our own physiology in mechanistic terms, such that medical intervention would parallel that of an engineer fixing a broken machine.

Technoscientific culture

The Enlightenment project, commencing in the eighteenth century, is still with us. By this we mean that the promises of scientific knowledge, as opposed to religious knowledge, are being extended and fulfilled with every new generation of discoveries. Rationalism, the belief in the use of reason to deduce knowledge claims with certainty, and empiricism, the belief in the use of experimental data to induce knowledge claims that are repeatable, have served us to overthrow superstition. Whether we recall the works of Francis Bacon, René Descartes or Immanuel Kant, we remain indebted to three centuries of progress in our knowledge base. Although we have modified their original claims, the spirit of the scientific model still guides us today.

The scientific model carried much weight because of its ability to communicate to the public a certain level of integrity and thereby enjoy the patronage of others in the way the arts enjoyed them in the Renaissance, for example (see Gillispie 1960: 109). As Robert Merton reminds us, the strengths of the scientific enterprise and the values adopted by its practitioners could sway any sceptic to join or support them. The scientific community valued and at times invited the open scrutiny of its research and publications (peer review), a certain level of fraternity or collegiality (appreciating collaboration for the sake of studying vast amounts of data), a notion of universalism or internationalism that transcended geographical and demographic boundaries and as such was less discriminatory than other organizations or institutions, and a great deal of freedom of thought from the state and the church, from anyone in position of authority (Merton 1973: Ch. 13). In some sense, the scientific enterprise became the prototype of the Enlightenment ideals in so far as it advocated equality and freedom, accepting more than rejecting the ideas of those who under previous circumstances of the learned societies were excluded.

One can recall in this context the words of Ernst Mach (1838–1916), one of the fathers of logical positivism, a powerful European movement between the two world wars devoted to simplification and precision in reporting natural facts and assembling them into meaningful protocol sentences that could easily be tested against natural phenomena:

> The belief in occult magic powers of nature has gradually died away, but in its place a new belief has arisen, the belief in the magical power of science. Science throws her treasures, not like a capricious fairy into the laps of a favored few, but into the laps of all humanity, with a lavish extravagance that no legend ever dreamt of! Not without apparent justice, therefore, do her distant admirers impute to her the power of opening up unfathomable abysses of nature, to which the senses cannot penetrate. Yet she who came to bring light into the world, can well dispense with the darkness of mystery, and with pompous show, which she needs neither for the justification of her aims nor for the adornment of her plain achievements.
>
> (Brody & Capaldi 1968: 15–16)

This belief in the powers of science has overshadowed any scepticism that could have been levelled against anything scientific. Regardless of our deep appreciation of the limits of scientific or medical knowledge, we still hold on to a belief in rationality itself as a principle and method by which we organize our data collection and with which we can be better armed, epistemologically speaking, to handle new natural phenomena and occurrences. Coupled with useful technological applications, science becomes an even more powerful ideal in the eyes of the western public, and because of this, the belief in the power of science and technology is compounded.

Those of us who prefer the term technoscience follow the advice of Jean-François Lyotard (1984) and Bruno Latour (1990), who insist that the old-fashioned division between science and technology is no longer operative in the twentieth century. Technology is not limited to the practical implementation of scientific theories, because technology is constitutive of the theoretical construction of scientific models (see Hesse 1966). Some of the greatest scientific achievements are indebted to the use of sophisticated equipment that could test theoretical speculations and turn them into scientific data (from the telescope to the laser). To speak of technoscience, then, is to speak about the interplay and interwoven nature of science and technology. More specifically, there are some researchers who observe, sociologically speaking, the linguistic and ideological underpinnings of specific scientific moves and discoveries (Latour 1987).

In a similar way, we speak today of postmodernism as a parallel tendency and attitude that accompanies our faith in modernism (regardless of how unfamiliar or misunderstood this term remains today). Modernism in its scientific constellation required the use of reason, rationality and logic so as to be able to provide objective, value-neutral and precise formulations of knowledge claims. By contrast, postmodernism, in the technoscientific realm, acknowledges the infusion of human biases, multiple interpretations of laboratory claims, the dynamic as opposed to static character of knowledge acquisition and the exogenous or environmental influences that enter into the constitution and presentation of such claims and data. Postmodernism in this context provides a broader appreciation that every technoscientific narrative is valuable and can contribute to a richer knowledge base for humanity. In opening its epistemological door, so to speak, to as many sources of knowledge as possible, it also acknowledges that there might not be a so-called metanarrative that encompasses all the narratives, that provides one uniform foundation, or one unique explanatory principle for any and all knowledge claims. At least in our appropriation of the term, this does not mean that anything goes or that there are no boundaries at all to knowledge claims (as some have suggested in the case of Paul Feyerabend (1975) in his view of epistemological anarchism). They might be esoteric and uncommon, they might be striking and unconventional, but as long as they make sense and can be communicated to or tested by others, they can be valuable and useful, and enlighten and enrich our knowledge base.

The fragmentation of human knowledge and the ongoing revisions we keep on making even to the most fundamental of our technoscientific beliefs have contributed to maintaining an open mind with regard to everything we know. We insist on a sceptical and critical approach in reviewing any piece of information about our environment and ourselves, especially when we deal with the biological sciences and the practice of medicine. We, therefore, must recognize that political pressures and economic conditions play an integral role in the development, acceptance or rejection and success or failure of any technoscientific model, as was the case with the national acceptance and eventual rejection of the Superconductor Supercollider designed to test scientific data in Texas (Sassower 1997). This does not mean that political pressures and economic conditions determine what we know and what we do; instead, it means that at times we focus on one area of research or treatment more carefully because of funding than on another less funded area.

With this in mind, we can begin to realize that general perceptions concerning technoscience are bound to be more complex than under a modernist conception that was more linear and universal in its appeal. Cultural settings, for example, have much to do with the application and expectations associated with technoscience even in the areas of transportation and communication, not to mention health care. For example, the economic support and financial incentives appropriated for the Human Genome Project to analyse and identify sequences of genes was a public undertaking with the support of the National Institutes of Health, but was also attempted by private corporations who claimed to be more efficient and less costly. In the political context these parallel attempts had economic factors associated with them (funding and eventual licensing fees) as well as legal ones (copyright issues associated with basic research of natural phenomena rather than techniques of application). This is not to say that the principles of gravity are relative to the cultures in which they are applied, but instead to realize that they might be interpreted differently under different cultural conditions and the conditions of intergalactic travel.

Contemporary claims associated with health care range from genetically engineered foods to the mapping of the human genome. Monsanto, one of the largest food suppliers in the world, boasts of having implemented new technologies in over one hundred million acres so that the dawn of a technological revolution in growing crops is apparent in the western diet (Specter 2000). This revolution has an effect on our food supplies and on the promise of overcoming starvation in this century and this obviously relates to health. Obviously questions relating to the fair distribution of foodstuff around the world must be addressed, but the very notion of abundance rather than scarcity is within human reach. The assumptions of scarcity and abundance might be relegated to the arena of neoclassical and Marxist economic models (Marx 1961), but they remain germane to a discussion about our outlook in contemporary culture. They turn out to be useful for any argument about the allocation of resources, the capitalist worldview of the ownership of the modes of production, distribution means and consumption patterns (Sassower 1990b).

As we proceed with claims associated with health, we also encounter a broader question concerning the environmental impact on health. We have shifted in the past century from a focus on individual health issues, by forerunners like Thomas Sydenham (1981), to an appreciation of studying public health. We have found out that food consumption, cleanliness and the transmission of disease through blood supplies, needle exchange and sexual behaviour have as much to do with the well-being of the individual as anything else. In the age of public health, the individual is only part of the focus and as such only part of the solution:

some procedures are covered by insurance policies, like triple bypass, and some are not, like hair transplant; some we spend funds to educate people about, like not smoking, and some we ignore, like not drinking on aeroplanes. There are public funds for education, like teaching children to brush their teeth, and for prevention, like prenatal care, just as there are for care, like kidney dialysis. At times funding is conditioned by politically or socially motivated agendas, such as when young women seeking abortion are discouraged from doing so and told of other alternatives. There are US states where underage women are legally required to consult their parents about abortion. The shift in emphasis from the individual to the community turns out to be a shift in the outlook of the individual who is seeking treatment with regard to what to expect from health care providers (Le Fanu 2000).

No longer do we consider the workings of researchers and clinical physicians in isolation from the broader culture in which they all work. As such, we ask questions about the culture in which we live, the expectations we have and the policies we implement to deal with health issues. The shift we examine here is postmodern in nature because it requires a multifaceted approach, one that considers the developments in science and technology to be important but not exclusive. It is in this sense that we label our approach integrative bioethics: a way to think about the scientific research of biological entities, the way we practise medicine and deploy certain technologies and innovations, as well as the way we think about the welfare of patients as consumers and as citizens, as friends and family members, in short, as people whose health is worthy of care.

The postmodern turn we have in mind is related to some of the tenets associated with this way of thinking. For us, postmodernism is not a periodizing exercise that tries to show how modernism is overshadowed by a new way of thinking. Instead, it is the infusion of a complementary way of thinking that critically approaches the excesses and shortfalls of modernism. Instead of proclaiming an objective and universal status to any technoscientific claim, the postmodern turn explains more patiently that there are always exceptions to the technoscientific rule. There are always situations and conditions that make any rule context-bound. This does not mean that the rule loses its value as a model with tested principles; only that it serves as a guide tolerant of changes and revisions. Moreover, the postmodern turn takes into consideration variables commonly left out of the technoscientific equations, such as alternative models and so-called pseudoscientific knowledge claims. In the area of medicine this would include alternative healing practices, herbal and psychological treatments, spiritual and shamanistic consultations and any other related activities. Finally, this postmodern turn makes sense in the twenty-first century because it integrates theory and practice, illustrating how technoscience is indeed a constellation of science and technology, with pure theoretical research and engineered applications and technical innovations.

When we advocate the notion of technoscience, we acknowledge the mutual dependence of the two areas and the collapse of one into the other. Scientific breakthroughs are intimately linked with technological innovations, some of which are premeditated and some of which are accidental, and technological instruments express a theoretical idea or speculation. This was true of ancient Egypt during the flooding of the Nile and the development of geometry, and this was also true of the development of the atomic bomb by the participants of the Manhattan Project. Technoscience is also a way to express the limits of the scientific model as envisioned by the Enlightenment leaders, for it discloses the practical mess that brings about or ensues with each theoretical novelty. It also demonstrates the irrational choices made by the technoscientific community when there is a paradigm shift, as Ludwik Fleck (1979) and Thomas Kuhn (1970) admit. Technoscientists themselves do not work in a vacuum, and they have financial and administrative pressures to perform specific tasks, with deadlines and budgets in mind. It is in this sense, then, that Michael Polanyi (1966) understood the need to speak of the scientific community rather than of science alone, and of the idea of "tacit knowledge" rather than only explicit knowledge found in textbooks and professional reports. Although Polanyi did not think of himself as postmodern in any sense of the term, he fits into our characterization of the postmodern turn in technoscience, because he shifts our focus from disembodied knowledge claims to the community of scientists whose work we tend to examine separately from them. Incidentally, this shift draws from Marxian notions of the bourgeois interest in formulating economic models and theories in particular ways that promote the interests of the bourgeoisie as well as from more contemporary concerns with "situated knowledge" expressed by some feminists, such as Donna Haraway (1991). It is, in short, a sociological turn as well.

When we speak of the postmodern technoscientific community, we invoke the influence of many more variables that hinder or promote progress. These variables are unrelated to the technical details of the technoscientific model, as was the case with the abandonment of the Superconductor Supercollider project in Texas in the early 1990s. Political pressures, financial limits and advocacy for motivating young researchers in the field all came to play an important part in how the project proceeded before Congressional committees considering its funding. All of these variables and the internal workings of the technoscientific community (with power plays and hierarchies) could be construed as irrational in contrast to the rational methods applied by technoscience. If there is an irrational element in the progress of technoscience, as Kuhn already conceded when describing revolutionary paradigm shifts, then how are we to assess medicine as a technoscientific endeavour? Moreover, if technoscience itself depends on a technoscientific community, and if the workings of this community can be deemed postmodern or arational (by classical standards of rationality), then how can we count on medicine to proceed rationally?

Now that we have established the problems associated with the scientific (rational and experimental) status of technoscience and, by extension, of medicine, it would make sense to approach the field of health care from a broader perspective than was the custom in the twentieth century. This would mean paying more attention to the cultural belief of a society and to the expectations that are raised within that culture. For example, the use of placebos in the administration of treatment has never been fully explained, especially if those receiving only sugar pills happen to be positively affected (Talbot 2000). As already mentioned earlier, another set of examples can be drawn from the use of so-called alternative treatments, namely eastern techniques and herbal medication, prayer or meditation and healing. The simple cause and effect model of medical treatment is challenged when research shows that hope plays an important and, at times, crucial role in the fight of the immune system.

As our western culture becomes less confident in the delivery of "cures" through long-established methods, and more interested in alternatives, medicine as we have known it will be changing as well. Surgical procedures for heart disease and cancer are not only perfected through smaller incisions and less invasive techniques, such as performed by laser, but are being questioned altogether. Are there healing methods we have not even tried yet? Will a change in diet radically change our approach to dealing with diseases only after the fact as opposed to preventing them? These questions are broadly construed questions that can be deemed cultural or social or philosophical and are related to public health education as much as they are questions about what an individual should or should not do. As such, they help in shifting the debate from the narrow confines of the efficacy of medicine as technoscience to the postmodern setting in which medical problems arise and are treated.

Public expectations: from the Nuremberg Trials to IRBs

Our expectations of health care provision have changed over time, and they keep on changing. These expectations change with time because the products and results experienced in this field keep on changing. For example, in neonatal care in intensive care units, the weight of a foetus at which there is minimal life expectancy shifted from under 1 kilogram to less than 500 grams in less than a decade (during the 1980s). By now, then, we expect that any foetus in the second trimester can be saved, even if the life of the mother is in danger. We put more pressure on physicians and hospitals to make available such results, no matter whether they indeed have the equipment and the experience to be successful. Expectations are heightened regardless of costs because there are implicit assumptions concerning the unquestionable value and sacredness of human life. Medicine is supposed to perform miracles no matter what financial or technical obstacles might hinder such a performance.

Instead of blaming the medical profession's infatuation with the culture of technoscience (the ability, as stated above, to have equipment with which to save underweight foetuses), we might profit by examining the conditions under which the profession has been practising in the past few years. We contend that it is public perception and expectation that have radically shifted of late and that contribute to the undue pressure on and confusion of health care provision. We do not mean to be prophets of doom and gloom, only critics who may offer a provisional explanation of this change of heart. With the introduction of the Internet, every patient is potentially more informed about her or his condition than ever before. We say potentially because the available data are provided out of context, without the benefit of the particular set of circumstances relevant to a particular patient. But the patient still feels empowered enough to question and at times challenge the general practitioner or the specialist, which might set an adversarial relationship with the health provider. How is this situation different from and more alarming than the one we witnessed only three decades ago?

We want to step back in history in order to ask this question. Those who know anything about the Nuremberg Trials that took place after the Second World War in order to try to indict those responsible for "crimes against humanity" usually have images of Nazi officers facing their acts of horror in western-style tribunals. Only part of what we heard then and from which we have benefited now has to do with the medical experimentations that were carried out in concentration camps. In the classic collection of essays edited by George J. Annas and Michael A. Grodin, the contributors explain the background that led to the ethical codes that are in place (and should have been) with regard to human experimentation.

Robert Proctor, for example, in his explanation of "racial cleansing" and the kind of "preventive medicine that was used by the Americans first, and then by the Germans, points out the continuity between theory and practice in the policies of the Germans" (Annas & Grodin 1992: 25), and their "effort to *biologize* or *medicalize* a broad range of social problems, including crime, homosexuality, the falling birth rate, the collapse of German imperial strength, and the Jewish and Gypsy 'problems'" (*ibid.*: 27). Proctor reminds us that the German doctors found little resistance to their agenda because their ideas and practices fit within a broad acceptance of the supremacy and validity of reductionist scientific knowledge. As long as medical practice was structured along "scientific" methods, there could be no reproach. Anything that could be legitimized in scientific terms could be easily translated into state policies.

Along these lines of argument, Christian Pross emphasizes how health policies in Germany were both scientifically approached and dealt with as the laws of the land – namely, having scientific and legal foundations. He also makes the following point: "What for you today appears contradictory in the nature of Nazism was the reason for its success: the connection between destruction and modernization" (Annas & Grodin 1992: 32). Pross makes another important point that the German model was blatant about two issues that affected its physicians: "an inflated application of machinery . . . seduces the physician who is permanently confronted with an imperfect, unpredictable human being to escape into the apparently safe world of laboratory parameters and computer scans" (*ibid.*: 39). And the other "was the tension between the physicians' fantasies of omnipotence and their factual impotence" (*ibid.*).

If we wish to follow the Nuremberg Code, Grodin's genealogy of the code is useful (*ibid.*: Ch. 7) and the three major principles that guide it are:

1   The voluntary consent of the individual upon whom the experiment is to be performed must be obtained.
2   The danger of each experiment *must* be previously investigated by animal experiments.

3 The experiment *must* be performed under proper medical protection and management.   (Annas & Grodin 1992: 134)

Lest we believe that these principles have become part of our legal system, Grodin cautions: "the Nuremberg Code remains more a statement of ethics than of law in the United States" (*ibid.*: 148). Likewise, in relation to the first Declaration of Helsinki (1964), Jay Katz reminds us that "the integrity of the scientific enterprise comes first, though it must be balanced against unspecified 'interests of the subject'" (*ibid.*: 231). Later Katz continues to say: "Scientific advances may be impeded, perhaps even become impossible at times, but this is a price worth paying" in order to abide by the spirit and the letter of the principles underlying the Nuremberg Code of ethics (*ibid.*: 236). Oddly enough, Arthur Caplan reminds us that one of the rationales offered at the doctors' trial was "that scientists and doctors are not responsible for and have no knowledge of values. They are only responsible for discovering and explaining empirical facts" (*ibid.*: 267). One could see here an invocation of the philosophical doctrine of logical positivism as a defence of the Nazi doctors' position, wherein all metaphysical and many ethical pronouncements are deemed beyond analysis and as such are logically or epistemologically meaningless.

It is this backdrop of the period after the Second World War that alerted patients to their rights and to the potential drawback of accepting physicians' authority (scientific and medical alike) on faith. By the 1960s more and more patients wanted to become involved in their own care and the care of their beloved, and this led to the patients' rights movement, which in fact helped to take care of many problems plaguing medicine. For example, paternalism (the view that parents and by proxy or extension medical experts as well know what is in the best interest of their child and therefore need not consult the child) was undermined, so that patients are consulted and have the right to question the medical authority. This means in some cases getting a second opinion. This also means having access to medical records and the translation of obscure technical language into the vernacular. This also means that patients must authorize any procedure they undergo and be convinced that it is in their best interest. Informed consent forms have been developed to accomplish this protection of patients' rights. After the 1960s, the patients' rights movement was a logical extension of the fight for the protection of our civil rights. As George Annas sees it, his role is writing a weekly column for the *Hastings Center Report* so as to address in a timely fashion specific medical issues, crises and concerns. His main concern is with patients' rights and "attempting to humanize the hospital environment through various strategies like statements of patients' rights" (Annas 1988: 1). Obviously, informed consent is high on his list. A lawyer by training, he anchors these rights in the legal framework that he is trying to find applicable in this context. Of interest to us might be some of his comments on institutional review boards (IRBs), especially on the lack of impact they have had on actual practice (*ibid.*: 331–3).

The mention of IRBs is relevant here since they provide a government-level realization of the need to monitor medical research and ensure the protection of patients. The IRBs' mandate takes the Nuremberg Code literally and tries to implement this as public policy in research institutions and for the pharmaceutical industry. Having an oversight committee of one's peers and of representatives from the public at large would, we hope, ensure that abuse is prevented, and the best interest of patients remains the focus of the discussion of approval or refusal to approve any medical protocol. Since both of us are veterans of these committees, having served for years on their boards, we have some personal experience with these procedures. Although in most cases philosophers are asked to contribute their suggestions to the wordings of informed consent forms (now mandatory before any medical procedure commences in medical institutions), we found ourselves being more interested in the methodology employed by the researchers. It should be noted here that IRB members are ostensibly responsible for assessing ethical issues and not scientific and methodological ones. But it is this separation between respons-ibilities or between areas of research and interest that we try to debunk or undermine here, for we find them to be interdependent.

Although we derived the position independently of each other (and because we served on boards in different states), nonetheless we agreed that our own informed judgement for approval or denial had to do with informal judgements of risk assessment, namely the ratio between benefits and harms that such a procedure might bring about. The methodology would affect, for example, the very appropriateness of carrying out the experiment: is the sample large enough? Is the method of inquiry commensurate with the data to be used? Should one proceed with the protocol given collected data that do not support any substantial efficacy of treatment? These questions must be addressed, in our view, in order to render a reasonable judgement about risks and benefits; if there is no conceivable benefit, then any risk whatsoever (emotional and psy-chological, not to mention physical) is not worth taking. Ethical considerations as such are thereby dependent on choices and deci-sions about epistemology (what we know and how we know what we know).

How, then, is the involvement of patients today different? Access to medical databases could be beneficial for patients if they under-stood how to use the data. Being informed is always better than not being informed, but how to interpret data, how to contextualize data and how to relate them to special cases are all difficult tasks that resist short cuts and simple answers. If the assumption is that the data are not corrupt, that they lead to clear-cut solutions and that all cases are alike, then there would be no problem and every patient could easily become her or his own health care advocate. But specialists do perform an essential role in translating general claims and applying them to particular cases. This is not to say that patients should not critically evaluate the judgements rendered by medical professionals. Instead, they should appreciate the points we made earlier in terms of the inherent limits to our knowledge claims, and the culture of entitlement in which we live.

Let us close this section by elaborating briefly on the notion of entitlement. The technoscientific culture promises to fix our ailments as if they were all mechanical in nature. Our car breaks down, and we know it can be fixed. Our energy resources are depleted, and we can develop alternative energy sources and restrain our consumption. We live in a postmodern culture that believes in the modernist view of the inevitability of human progress and the perfectibility of the human mind. Our expectations with regard to health care are culturally treated as if they were no different from the expectations regarding nuclear power: deep down everything has a technoscientific fix. But what if the human body and the environment with which it interacts are not so easily reduced to treatable variables? What if the level of complexity dictates that each individual be treated differently from any other? What if there are no models to use as guides for *all* cases? What if we need to use multiple contexts for each individual so as to have more definitive answers to our questions?

These questions should put a dent in a culture that believes in the promises of the Enlightenment project and their latest incarnations. We may not be entitled to a simple answer or to a simple cure, because our case falls outside any previously experienced situation. Technoscientific knowledge and prowess do not entitle us to anything but a critical and humble approach to health care provision. Perhaps some would consider us lucky for having almost doubled our life expectancy in the past century, but this does not entitle us to immortality. It only entitles us to participate in the wonders and difficulties of medicine and appreciate the uncertainties that are inherent in it for a longer period of time.

Perhaps ours is a postmodern culture that is modernist enough to insist on fast food solutions to our hunger, a perfectly predictable meal, prepared with identical ingredients, wrapped and sold in identical venues, all under the watchful eye of quality control engineers. But modernist solutions that dictate predictability might not be applied in the field of health care, where a postmodern reality is less comforting, but might be a more accurate representation of the human condition. We cannot go to the clinic or the hospital and expect to be immediately "fixed". We cannot go to college and expect to be educated. In both cases, we have to realize that we are not spectators but active participants in our own treatment. We contribute to what is done with us and to us; and as active contributors, we should change our expectations of the other – the doctor, the nurse, the surgeon – and begin to focus on ourselves.

We wish to end our comments with some general statements about the future of health care provision at least in the United States. Some of these comments might translate well into other contexts, some will not. First, the increased expectations of the present century with regard to health care provision, whether we relinquish the notion of entitlement or not, will not diminish soon. Instead, we keep on expecting that technoscience will come up with easy "fixes" to all our ailments for less and less money. How each individual interprets these expectations in terms of the meaning of life and what values are ascribed to the quality of each individual life cannot be summarized here. Perhaps such a summary cannot and should not be attempted, for in doing so we might inadvertently offend someone's views, beliefs or dreams and aspirations. Perhaps it is best left to the individual to determine what should or should not be expected from health care providers and public health.

Secondly, if we are serious about considering the individual as part of a community, then we ought to recognize the interdependence of people living in a community. By this we mean not only how we transmit diseases, but also how we are socially organized. Our social standing, our income and wealth, play a vital role in the prevention of ill-health and the provision of and access to health care. We must reconsider whether this is a zero-sum game where those who benefit more from the distribution of medical goods and services do so at the expense of others.

Thirdly, if we consider the community in terms of health care rather than the treatment of particular diseases, then we ought to be more open to environmental considerations. We are thinking here of pollution, water consumption, living conditions, modes of transportation, addictive habits and even gun control. We should recall that our statistical databases all include death rates associated with our lifestyle and cultural settings, and are not limited to infections and traumas. So, if we speak of medicine, we should speak of all of the variables that contribute to the health of our community.

Fourthly, if we agree to speak of postmodern technoscience as the culture that guides the theoretical and practical aspects of health care provision, then we ought to provide multiple models to discuss the problems associated with health care provision in an interdisciplinary manner so as to integrate all the relevant components we have discussed all along. We should never adopt only one model, but insist on the critical presentation of complementary or alternative models of treatment. We should provide all the data we can to our health care providers so that what might seem secondary could be considered as well, because it may turn out to be a crucial variable that determines the efficacy of the treatment of our condition.

Finally, although sceptical and critical to the core, our approach to health care should also be seen as humble and grateful. For the great progress over the past 100 years has helped to alleviate pain and suffering for millions of people around the globe, and has allowed us to enjoy a quality of life we could not have imagined possible only five generations ago. Medical pioneers, researchers and clinicians alike, as well as patients and research subjects, ought to be commended for the personal sacrifices they have made and continue to make in the name of the care and cure of patient complaints. Lest we forget, they remain our most humble servants who put their own life at risk more often than we know. What have we done in return? When was the last time we publicly thanked them?

2

Medical epistemologies and goals

This chapter is devoted to a reconstruction of the history of medicine so as to draw attention to the promises and shortcomings of clinical medicine. We will include some of the debates among physician-philosophers about the nature of disease (as a cornerstone of medicine) discussed by Hippocrates and Galen, as well as later debates in modern Europe involving, for example, Sydenham and Sauvages, Morgagni and Boerhaave, Bichat and Virchow, and Harvey and Semmelweis. Our brief and cursory survey of some of these debates is undertaken with the explicit motivation of illustrating the extent to which the very framing of these debates highlights the reciprocity between theory and practice. By this we mean how one's practice informs one's knowledge, and, likewise, how one's knowledge informs one's practice. This reciprocity may seem transparent from a contemporary perspective when we realize that science is not purely theoretical or that technology, for example, is intimately concerned with its theoretical foundation. But in the past, the participants in these debates would overlook their theoretical prejudices and consider them obvious or irrelevant. Likewise, clinical insights were informed by one's culture and set of beliefs, so that some "facts" were more readily observed than others. The intricacies of these historical contexts impose a lengthy discussion that goes beyond a simple framing of the process of knowing and valuing medical knowledge and treatment.

This chapter is meant not as a historical overview, but as a way to reintroduce some of the perennial issues that plague us today. In the age of scientific progress, it seems that the past has been overcome, that whatever speculative confusions we held on to in history, have once and for all been clarified by the dawn of the twenty-first century. But postmodernity teaches us to go back to alleged dead ends of the past in order to find pearls of wisdom and folk remedies whose efficacy is astounding. When doing so, we end up with a plurality of views that can be used integratively as opposed to discarding one in order to use another. In the case of medicine, we end up with frameworks for knowing, doing and valuing that address what we know, how we know it and what we are going to do in the light of our knowledge. This takes time and patience.

Historical frameworks and buried insights

In studying medicine, one is introduced to the rich domain of philosophy. Medicine embraces a wide range of endeavours that apply scientific generalizations to the care and cure of medical problems patients bring to the attention of health care professionals. Broadly speaking, medicine involves not only what physicians do, but also the intellectual and clinical endeavours of doctors of optometry, podiatry, chiropractors, as well as of nurses, physician assistants, health care administrators, pastoral counsellors and allied health professionals. Medicine can and often does refer to the basic sciences (e.g. theories about the way the eye functions) and applied endeavours tied to diagnosis (e.g. retinitis pigmentosa), prognosis (e.g. deterioration of vision over a certain period of time) and treatment (e.g. drugs or low vision therapy). As a result, one may engender puzzles about theories of function and models of disease processes (e.g. as found in the physiology, pathology and genetics of the eye), about the ways in which health care practitioners engage in their diagnostic, prognostic and therapeutic activities (e.g. the ways ophthalmologists and optometrists make clinical judgements), about how patients assimilate clinical information (e.g. deciding whether to accept pharmaceutical or behavioural intervention) and how social and economic factors influence the understanding and treatment of disease (e.g. how insurers structure reimbursements for eye care). In this way, medicine is, as Engel (1977) puts it, a biopsychosocial discipline, as already noted in Chapter 1.

But medicine is more than a study of the human as object, because humans cannot fully be explained in terms of third person language. Purpose, value, consciousness, reflection, fear and self-determination complicate the laws of medicine. Medicine must consider the special complexities of the human as an individual subject of his or her self-perceived history. In so doing, it must correlate the explanatory modes of the physical sciences with the interpretive modes of the humanities (Pellegrino 1976: 15; see also Cutter 2003). It must take into consideration the special complexities of humanity as a biological species that is the product and producer of its environments.

In this view, medicine is rooted in the history and traditions of philosophies and cultures. The following geography of medical history is offered in order to illustrate a range of explanations of disease that medicine provides. It is not to be taken as a *definitive* set of explanations or views of medical progress. It is simply a broadly construed summary of distinct kinds of explanations of disease that have been handed down in medicine and that have guided the development of medical interventions. We address at greater length in the section "Contextualizing medical reality" below and again in Chapter 4 our approach to dealing with conflicts between and among different clinical explanations and interventions.

It is interesting to note that "prehistoric" or "primitive" (Hudson 1983) medicine, the medicine of the earliest civilizations, for instance, assumes a supernatural view of disease, one in which disease results from punishment or possession by supernatural forces or the forces of sorcery (*ibid.*: 59–60). One is reminded of stories from early mythologies of possession by evil forces that account for human disease or dysfunction and its treatments. This approach provides the solace of explanation when the human mind cannot understand the nature of disease, or control its course, or find any appreciable pattern in those afflicted.

Ancient Greek medicine (approx. 500BCE–500CE) offers a naturalist, as opposed to a supernaturalist (Laín-Entralgo 1970; Amundsen 1977), approach to disease. This is a monumental shift in the perception of the world in general and of medical practice in particular. When one looks to nature, one can find all the answers one is looking for. If one looks carefully enough, one can discover or uncover the general structure of disease. Once that is accomplished, without shamans and appeal to the gods, one can be in a better position, as a physician or caretaker, to outline or propose instructions for remedies and therapies. If one practises this way of dealing with diseases long enough and collects medical reports, some generalization can be developed and eventually used by others. When faced with failure, it is not because the gods are angry or because the sacrifices offered to them were insufficient, it is because we overlooked some natural experiences or variables or generalized too carelessly.

Hippocrates (fifth century BCE) (1943) offers a powerfully influential account of disease in terms of generalized imbalances of the fluid portion of the body, namely the four humours (blood, phlegm, yellow bile and black bile), which correspond to the four elements (earth, water, fire and air). Now this might sound like a bizarre way of looking at our health or the diseases that inflict us, yet it is a radical change from the appeal to supernatural forces with which we cannot negotiate or that we do not fully understand (Hudson 1983: 82). Once the issue of bodily balance or equilibrium is recognized as the foundation of understanding diseases, treatment is more rationally designed and focused around balancing the fluid portions of the body. Hippocrates' account of epilepsy, or "sacred disease", for example, challenged previous supernatural accounts (despite the continued use of the adjective "sacred") and provided a remarkably enduring account of the clinical signs and symptoms usually associated with epilepsy. Without going into great detail, any practising physician today could use these alleged ancient descriptions and immediately recognize the phenomenon when the terms remain obscure or outdated.

Although the Hippocratic view of disease is rooted in observation and the accumulated experiences of physicians, we notice that Galen (131–201) is profoundly interested in the theoretical foundation of medicine. We contend, in fact, that his view is a precursor to that of Kant (1724–1804), who pulls together the insights and contributions of the empiricists and the rationalists. Instead of maintaining that only observations and experiences drive our understanding and the progress of knowledge or that logic alone can steer us away from the misguided and false collection of data, Galen (like Kant after him) appreciated the need to combine both. Once data are collected, they have to be rationally analysed and classified; once logic is introduced, it becomes a tool for the study of our experiences with patients and their medical conditions. Galen even divided the contesting views of his days with terms such as "empiricists", "rationalists", "dogmatics" and "methodists". What is fascinating is the fact that these terms translate quite easily into contemporary debates and reveal Galen's concern with any sort of reductionism – the view that there is one and only one set of principles or ideas with which to approach any and all medical phenomena.

As we push forward into the medieval period, there is a certain reversal in the appeal to supernatural or divine forces. Judaeo-Christian-Islamic scholars, although appreciating the naturalistic shift in the view of medicine that preceded them, find the congeniality between the knower and the known and the discovery of grand patterns fortified by the will of their Abrahamic God, thus leading medicine again to embrace supernatural accounts of disease. But this time, the supernatural is a theistic entity that is both singular and to a great extent rational. It is under these changed circumstances that one can have a personal relationship with the divine so that one knows (for sure) what is expected and for what reasons one might be punished (with, for instance, disease). Maimonides the Jew (1135–1204), Al-Gazali the Muslim (1058–1111) and St Augustine the Christian (354–430) share a similar foundation even when the specific language or examples they use might differ. Consider in Psalm 103 the following: "Praise the Lord, O my soul . . . who forgives all your sins and heals all your diseases" (2–3). Or in Luke 9:1 the following: "Then Jesus had called the Twelve together, he gave them power and authority to drive out all demons and to cure diseases" (*New International Version*). Supernatural accounts of disease as punishment for sins and possession by the devil, treatable by blessings from or sacrifices by a spiritual leader, reflect a view of the universe as created by God, governed by general natural law but faulted by evil influence (Wulff 1986: 81–3).

Classical modern medicine purportedly rejects speculative, metaphysical and faith-based accounts of disease, thus leading to a revival of naturalistic accounts of disease that use the metaphor of a machine. What should be emphasized at this juncture is the cyclical shifts in the approach to medicine: from supernatural explanations to natural ones, from natural to supernatural (though more sophisticated) ones and so on. Fuelling the ongoing shift in explanatory emphasis is a sort of scepticism regarding nonrational forms of knowledge and their capacity to grant reliable answers for those who have a disease. Although this scepticism appears as far back as Sextus Empiricus in the early third century, it gains wide acceptance with sixteenth- and seventeenth-century scholars, such as Bacon, Galileo and Descartes. Without surveying their arguments and contributions and the specific concerns they have had with their predecessors (e.g. Bacon and speculative statements about natural phenomena), we would like to suggest the following.

What is appealing in a modern mechanistic view of nature is the fact that we can have both a soft naturalistic and a soft supernaturalistic view because God created a perfect world that is ingeniously designed (like a machine, if you wish). The workings of the world, from its rotation and relation to the sun and the moon (whether understood biblically or astronomically), to the growth and development of humans and their environment, are not accidental. There is always an underlying purpose and a rational model of explanation. So, when we see a wild fire, we know that the ground was dry, that fire was lit and a wind blew in a certain direction. Likewise, when the body is seen as a machine (Harvey comes to mind as the proponent of blood circulation), and every element or part thereof has a particular role to play (like cogs in a machine or clock, as used to be the favourite example of the moderns), then any disease can be explained (in principle, if not in practice). This mechanistic view of nature carries through into the workings of medicine at the time, and therefore has all the advantages and problems associated with it. For example, what if nature is not a "machine" in some absolute sense of mechanism, but a more dynamic constellation of variables that themselves are prone to change (evolve, transform, merge)? It should be noted here that the mechanistic model is both explanatory and predictive in the sense of being useful for treatment. If this body part is infected, then this would be the result. If this is true, then we can intervene in specific ways to bring about specific medical results (alleviate symptoms, if possible, and on rare occasions have them disappear). God might have brought about this model and its functioning; but merely praying to him (as the medievalists thought they could do) might not be sufficient for the treatment of disease.

To talk about a modern mechanistic view of the world and of medicine is to talk about ordering the world and disease. Ordering, as Michel Foucault (1973) taught us, is itself a somewhat arbitrary endeavour. For example, one can say that all cows are divided into those that are owned by the king and those that are not. Likewise, in earlier times, Aristotle was considered the master of classification and in that sense of ordering. What we would like to illustrate at this historical juncture is the struggle with the ordering of disease and how this has affected the present time. The early moderns were still concerned with ordering in terms of symptoms, rather than aetiological (causal) origins. Consider the ten major classes under which François Boissier de Sauvages de Lacroix (1707–67) united forty-two orders, some 315 genera and 2400 diseases (depending on which edition one consults) (Sauvages 1768). For Sauvages and for others of his time, such as Thomas Sydenham (1624–89) and William Cullen (1710–90), fevers and pains were major classes of disease in their own right. Treatments targeted the symptoms, in the case of fever, heat, for which Peruvian bark was recommended. Phenomena were brought together in a way that might appear strange to many of our contemporaries because they neglected to account for the ways in which fever or pain related to its aetiological origins. Still, they were brought together and set the stage for the extensive development of clinical nosologies (clinical classifications) and clinical nosographies (clinical descriptions).

What makes classical modern medicine unique is not its shift from supernatural accounts of disease to natural accounts, for this is seen in earlier periods. What makes it unique is its shift from a generalized to a contextual account of disease – that is, from some idealized description and model of a disease (even when many instances were observed at some point) to an appreciation of the particular patient who is suffering from this or that disease (whose signs and symptoms may be expressed differently in each patient). Although this shift from generalized to localized notion of disease takes centuries, and is evolving even today, it clearly sees its infancy in the works of scientific anatomists Leonardo da Vinci (1452–1519) and Andreas Vesalius (1514–64), who focus not only on particular anatomical structures but on particular anatomical functions, which encourages developments in pathology (e.g. Giovanni Battista Morgagni, 1682–1771), physical diagnosis (e.g. Hermann Boerhaave, 1668–1738; René Théophile Hyacinthe Laënnec, 1781–1826), tissue pathology (Marie François Xavier Bichat, 1771–1802), cellular pathology (Rudolf Virchow, 1821–1902), surgery (e.g. John Hunter, 1728–93) and anaesthesia (e.g. Horace Wells, 1815–48).

With nineteenth-century developments in medicine and science, there occurs a transition in the ways in which clinical problems are explained. Fever and pain as such are no longer considered diseases in their own right, but symptoms associated with an underlying pathoanatomical and pathophysiologial basis or process. Clinical complaints that had not been previously associated with a particular disease could now be brought together under one rubric. For example, phthisis, scrofula, consumption, and Pott's disease could be reorganized as manifestations of tuberculosis. Aetiological accounts of the origin of pathoanatomical or pathophysiological findings also have an impact in distinguishing previously undiscriminated problems such as anaemia, which could now be distinguished as general, chronic splenic and pernicious. These changes lead to the notion that the goal of medicine is comprehending pathoanatomical and pathophysiological *underpinnings* of clinical problems, and merely reporting the symptoms is inadequate (Foucault 1973; Engelhardt 1996). Patient complaints of a specific symptom have to be examined in different ways so as to figure out how the symptoms relate to their own physical conditions, their general health and the functioning of all their organs, tissues and cells. Although symptoms are localized in the individual patient, there is still a general appreciation of the body as a whole, where each part affects all others.

Consider the extraordinary work of nineteenth-century clinician-scientists Ignaz Philipp Semmelweis (1818–65) (Sinclair 1932) and Robert Koch (1843–1910) (Koch 1932). Semmelweis's study of childbed fever that results in maternal death led him to conclude that the agents responsible for childbed fever are cadaveric particles passed from the sick and dead on the hands of medical attendants to healthy women (Hudson 1983: 146–53). An aetiological account of disease was more fully developed by Koch when he studied anthrax, a disease found in cattle. Following Koch's careful scientific work to map out the causal agent and its effects, late nineteenth- and early twentieth-century scientists identified the bacterial cause for many human diseases, such as cholera, diphtheria, typhoid, gonorrhoea, meningitis, tetanus and botulism. The stage was set for the development of treatments, such as penicillin for anthrax (around 1889) and sulphanilamide for pneumococcus (around 1938) (Hudson 1983: Ch. 8).

Contemporary or postmodern ways of understanding disease

arise from prior assumptions and question the legitimacy of a single narrative forwarded by modern clinicians and scientists. This means that the general, perhaps absolute, notions of disease (whether symptom- or organ-based) are replaced by more moderate and contextualized ways of describing patients' complaints. Instead of matching a complaint with a disease (as if one fits perfectly with the other), there is a more nuanced way of exploring the variables that contribute to one's complaints or that would make one category or class of disease more appropriate than another. This should not be mistaken as a way simply to discard the great wealth of knowledge accumulated over the years concerning the kind of classification and ordering in medicine. Nor should this mean that every patient is so individuated that no population-based data are relevant, thus leading to an extreme relativistic mode of diagnosing. Instead, there is a fine interplay between nature and nurture, between the so-called naturalistic views we have outlined above (as they are historically understood) and the supernaturalistic views that are now understood not in terms of angry gods or demons, but in cultural and historical (geographic and demographic) ones, and between the individual and the community.

As we have illustrated in Chapter 1, there are some contemporary scholars who find the nascent elements in this postmodern view of medicine already in Ludwik Fleck's work. For them, Fleck, and his successor Kuhn, as well as others like Foucault, pay much more attention than many others of their time to the historical, socially constructed and culturally determined character of science and medicine. What they have taught us is to pay attention to contextual accounts of disease, which means viewing the patient as a member of a group who still deserves personalized diagnosis. The differences between and among ethnic and gender groups (e.g. Ashkenazi Jews, Africans, northern Europeans) that are more prone to develop one kind of a disease as opposed to another (e.g. Tay-Sachs, sickle cell, cystic fibrosis, respectively) have become pronounced enough to demand a different explanation. That explanation itself can be, once again, reductionistic or more synergistic in the sense of pulling together relevant variables that may be deemed irrelevant on the face of it. For example, should one's Jewishness be a factor in a disease? When commonly asked, this question itself may seem anti-Semitic; yet it must be asked, given the long history of isolated, and at times intertribal, marriages among Jews. Similarly, it is not misogynistic to note that women might be more prone to encounter one kind of a disease (e.g. lupus) or be more affected by one set of conditions (e.g. alcohol) as opposed to another. The quandary, of course, is that we are faced with the primary question of the strict scientific status of medicine. And this, as we argue, is what interests and fascinates the post-modernists, following, as they do, the ancients.

To treat all patients as if they are identical is to overlook their differences. Whether these differences are considered essential or accidental is not what concerns us here. Instead, we note that different populations, however construed, deserve different contexts within which they ought to be studied and treated. This is true also when we bring to bear social and cultural identification or classification, such as race and ethnicity (e.g. Roberts 1996), class (e.g. Rothenberg 2001) and gender (e.g. Tuana 1988; Cutter 1997). Economic conditions that might not be the first to be observed when patients complain about symptoms might turn out to be crucial. What is their typical diet? What amount of alcohol and prescription drugs do they consume? How many cigarettes do they smoke? How much do they weigh? Are they living in a lead-painted home? It is with these variables that the local observation is enhanced and the treatment can be more effective. Lifestyle issues, such as smoking and obesity, correlate strongly with specific diseases. Ignoring these kinds of variables would obscure whatever other data clinicians collect and lead to poor health care provision. The Enlightenment project of modernity that exclusively emphasized the scientificity of medical care is being challenged by post-modernism so as to broaden the scope of gathering data and finding effective ways of dealing with medical ailments.

Nevertheless, all is not fractured. Put differently, we are not moving from an absolutist–foundational commitment to a relativistic–isolationist free-for-all. One need not discard everything of modernity when appreciating the nuances and opportunities afforded by postmodernism. The two philosophical approaches or meta-physical convictions can be simultaneously used. The technological revolution, undergirded by developments in information techno-logy, link previously isolated voices, communities and cultures. In doing so, they illustrate common grounds across cultural divides as well as a sea of difference that emerges only when we compare one set of data with another. We know immediately, for instance, where and when disease outbreaks occur (as in the cases of AIDS, severe acute respiratory syndrome or SARS and bird flu). Advocates for intervention go worldwide – with their voices (e.g. Bono, Angelina Jolie) and their funds (e.g. Bill Gates, Warren Buffet) – and organize campaigns to target particular medical issues. Scholars, philanthropists and nongovernmental organizations call for a transnational or global perspective (e.g. Tong *et al.* 2000; Po-wah 2002; World Health Association 2003) on matters concerning life and death. This is not merely a way of worrying about the spread of a disease and its "containment" at its source; instead, this belies an appreciation that even when the "same" disease looks different at another place, it may have "similar" markers or manifestation. The uniformity and universality that science promised in its modern dawn in its guise of anatomical structure and function or aetiological entity have been supplanted by a postmodern recogni-tion that age, gender, ethnicity and the environment matter. In a sense, going "global" has been misunderstood as a way to deal with differences in a sensitive manner (we should care about what hap-pens in Africa), because it in effect reverts to a modernist view of medicine and disease (everything is the same everywhere). By con-trast, what we advocate here is a different kind of "going global". For us, the global can be instructive for a "localized clinical episte-mology", because it adds new dimensions and layers of data that are applicable in each and every case (Cutter 2002a, 2003).

One consequence of this move to reject a grand narrative in medicine (in Lyotard's sense) is confusion. False promises are coupled with misguided expectations and lead to the spread of frustrations. Why can we not cure AIDS once and for all? Why can we not find a way to fight cancer? For that matter, why have we not found a simple cure for the common cold? Are we left with old wives' tales and chicken soup? Should we consider more seriously alternative medical treatments, such as homeopathic cures and acupuncture? If medicine is nothing but a field of scientific research, and if all scientific research is reducible to a set of variables that correlate one way or another with another set of variables, then the public perception is indeed that a big enough computer could (and should) find the algorithm to solve this or that question about this or that disease. But this is not the case. Medicine has become the battleground for competing scientific models and ideological convictions, because science itself is no longer considered a monolithic or homogeneous endeavour. On the one hand, we have intellectual prowess (in Condorcet's (1979) sense of human perfectibility) that is supposed, with sufficient funding, to discover all the secrets of the human body (if understood mechanistically), and on the other hand, we have a hodgepodge of models and practices that are sanctioned by the government health services and the insurance industry that allow "alternative", eastern healing and that are neither uniform nor universal. The individual is left to fend for herself in an environment that promises too much and delivers too little.

All of this is to underscore that a philosophical approach to medicine is unavoidable. The more one comes to understand the conceptual underpinnings of our ideas and actions in medicine, the more one can make sense out of the complexity of clinical reality and the more one can successfully manipulate it. We are reminded once again that medicine as an art and learned profession has much to gain from reflections in philosophy. And by this we mean not simply the practice of applied ethics but a broader study of epistemology and metaphysics. Along with law and religion, health care has traditionally been seen not merely as a technical or trades field, but as a profession that is sensitive to its own commitments and its responsibility to the culture at large.

Conversely, philosophy has much to learn from medicine. Discussions regarding reality or nature, those that focus on methods of knowing and those probing the boundaries of possible and permissible action are as central to philosophy as they are to medicine. Medicine offers endless examples of problems, resolutions and irresolvable quagmires that philosophers of science as well as ethicists and others concerned with ways of knowing can draw from. As laypersons become increasingly educated about medical matters, thanks in part to the Internet and media attention, traditional philosophical debates become accessible with examples drawn from medicine. Discussions regarding quality of life, understood in terms of economic factors and preference theory, gain new light when addressed from the standpoint of an actual case such as that involving Terri Schiavo (who, as a brain-damaged woman dependent on a feeding tube, became the centre piece of a national right-to-die battle). Medicine is a unique area of research and practice that sheds light on what we study in philosophy. The contested boundary conditions between science and technology, theory and practice, and science and art come to light when we speak of human ailments, diseases and treatments.

Theory and practice

Explanation is central to clinical medicine. In clinical medicine, explanation brings intelligibility to a wide range of clinical problems, complaints and symptoms expressed and displayed by patients. Explanatory models make sense of the clinical setting where patient meets doctor, where a vague complaint is analysed and classified, through the combination of our knowing and doing. Clinicians wish to establish through explanation the regularities of occurrences among clinical phenomena and to find simple and coherent models to account for these regularities. In this way, clinicians function as medical scientists seeking to know truly the facts that constitute the world of clinical problems. But even in this respect the scientific model itself must account for judgements regarding what goals patients seek (less pain, cure from future illness), what underlies the rationality of such goals (the cultural or social frameworks, related to concepts of health, longevity and quality of life) and what constitute appropriate means to achieve

51

such goals (intervention in the form of an operation or daily doses of prescribed drugs). In short, medical explanation involves a complex integration between knowing the fabric of clinical reality and the goals of human life particularly as they have to do with the mitigation, if not elimination, of patient complaints.

This dynamic interaction between knowing and doing informs both our knowledge base and our treatment of disease. The judgements we make about medical "facts" determine how effective the treatment turns out to be, where effectiveness is measured in monetary and non-monetary terms. Consider the case of coronary artery disease. The multiple factors in coronary artery disease suggest that the disease could be alternatively construed as a genetic, metabolic, anatomical, psychological or sociological disease, depending on whether one is a geneticist, general practitioner, surgeon, psychiatrist or public health official. The construal will depend upon the particular scientist's appraisal of which aetiological variables are most amenable to the clinician's manipulations. Put differently, as Friedrich Nietzsche has already taught us, one's perspective is crucial in determining what one sees, what one highlights and how one explains the reality that is observed. This, incidentally, does not mean that we know nothing or that what we know about the facts of the matter can be manipulated or twisted around by anyone at will. Instead, this means that it is important to appreciate the multiple explanatory models that inform each observer and that contribute to a fuller picture of the medical ailment and its eventual treatment. For example, a public health official may decide that the basic variables in coronary artery disease are elements of a lifestyle that includes little exercise, overeating and cigarette smoking. Alternatively, a surgeon will see the defining features of coronary artery disease as a clogged artery and restricted blood flow. Depending on whether one is a public health official or a surgeon, one will recommend lifestyle changes or surgical intervention, respectively.

The point here is that views regarding what it means to know truly and to intervene effectively can vary among communities of clinicians. As the contributions of Fleck and Kuhn to the history and philosophy of science have shown, there are no such things as neutral, naked or bare facts. Facts always appear interpreted within the embrace of theoretical frameworks, whether or not these frameworks are formally or informally developed as scientific accounts, and whether or not we are aware of them. In addition, they are always contextualized within a sociohistorical framework, where "unscientific" or exogenous variables are relevant. The modernist expectation of a timeless or transcendental account of medical reality is untenable because humans live in changing environments, which change them, too.

Fleck provides a vivid illustration of the development of the modern concept of syphilis from the early modern concept of "carnal scourge" to the mid-modern "empirical-pathological concept" (treatable with the nonspecific agent mercury) to the late modern "experimental-pathological concept" (treatable with the specific anti-bacterial agents arsphenamine and neoarsphenamine). At the end of the fifteenth century, syphilis was largely undifferentiated from other "carnal scourges" characterized by skin signs found in the genitals (e.g. gonorrhoea, soft chancre). Most clinicians assumed that the conjunction of Saturn and Jupiter under the sign of Scorpio and the House of Mars on 25 November 1484 was the cause of this condition. Benign Jupiter was vanquished by the evil planets Saturn and Mars. The sign of Scorpio, which rules the genitals, explained why the genitals were the first place to be attacked by the new disease. Additionally, some referred the cause of the disease to God, who had sent it as a punishment to mankind for the sin of fornication (Fleck 1979: 2–3). With the rise of empirical medicine, some witnessed the healing power of mercury in cases of syphilis, something that goes back to the ancients, and sought scientific or biological answers. The discovery of the causative agent, *Spirochaeta pallida*, together with the development of the Wasserman reaction as a diagnostic and effective antibacterial agents, helped to establish the late modern and contemporary concept of syphilis. In the course of time, then, the concept of syphilis changed "from the mythical, through the empirical and generally pathogenetical, to the mainly etiological" (*ibid.*: 19).

One does not have to look through the long history of medicine to witness the change in understanding of disease and its treatment. Take the late twentieth-century clinical condition acquired immunodeficiency syndrome (AIDS) (Cutter 2003: Ch. 2). In its inception in the early 1980s, AIDS was understood through phenomenological (sign-based and symptomatic) categories, namely skin lesions, fatigue, recurrent fevers, unintended weight loss, uncontrollable diarrhoea and skin rashes. Initial treatments included those already developed for fevers, weight loss and rashes. In the mid-1980s, AIDS came to be understood not as a syndrome (even though the name remained the same) but as an aetiological entity, with "HIV" being assigned as the cause and target for therapeutic intervention in 1985 (Varmus 1989). Despite the success of explanation, researchers continue to struggle to understand AIDS and create effective interventions in part because the "cause" changes (mutates), variations in the host are recognized and some interventions (e.g. preventive measures) are easier and/or less expensive to develop and administer than others (e.g. behavioural changes versus expensive drug "cocktails"). AIDS is seen as a multifactorial process, not the result of a unifactorial force. Medicine as a scientific model of explanation comes to appreciate the complexity of disease and its multiple interventions.

In talking about clinical explanation, then, one must identify the particular community of scientists to which one wishes to make reference. Each community is defined by its own rules of evidence, inference and negotiation. Scientists who are members of a particular community, as Polanyi and Kuhn have illustrated in their description of "tacit knowledge" and "paradigms", respectively, know which facts are important and why. They are trained and socialized in particular ways that channel their interests and their research, namely the information that they accept as relevant to their field. They know when particular facts fit their explanatory model and therefore warrant particular conclusions or particular interventions. In medicine, the rules of inference include recipes for action, which incorporate implicit, and at times explicit, value judgements about proper trade-offs among competing relevant facts and treatment options that will often be negotiated without a claim that absolutely correct answers are available. One might think here, for instance, of clinical classificatory schemes for cancer that form the basis not only for prognosis but also for different levels of therapeutic interventions. For example, in the 1980s, and in the case of squamous cell carcinoma, the rationale for combining severe dysplasia and carcinoma *in situ* into one category was that severe dysplasia and carcinoma *in situ* could not be consistently differentiated morphologically, and there was no known difference in biological behaviour between the two conditions. Moreover, since women with mild and severe dysplasia tended to be undertreated, clinicians offered a new classification reflecting a clinical approach that minimized over- and undertreatment, thus revising the classification for the Pap smear, introduced in the 1940s, which tests for the degree of preneoplastic lesion of the cervical and vaginal epithelium (Cutter 1992). In the end, women are more appropriately treated for squamous cell carcinoma.

It should be obvious that the classification of cancer is not like the classification of stars. The planetary rotation of stars remains unaffected when stars are assigned human-like characteristics and then claimed to be acting in certain ways that influence our life. In this sense, then, stellar motion is observed and can be independently tested from any perspective one chooses, just like the development of cancer cells. Yet there is a fundamental difference between one set of observations and another. The choice among different ways of classifying cancer sets the conditions for the ways in which physicians will choose therapeutic interventions (whereas no matter which astronomical model we choose, the stars will remain unaffected). The number of stages selected presupposes cost–benefit calculations and understandings of prudent actions that have direct implications for the ways in which patients are treated. They involve more than scientific judgements; they concern the proper balancing of benefits and harms in the organization of therapeutic choices around a particular number of stages of cancer. And this is the case not only for cancers, but for other clinical conditions. The choice to subdivide stages of cancer development will reflect the decision that a more complex assessment of therapeutic options is useful in terms of this or that particular intervention (chemotherapy, surgery or diet changes). Since the treatment of patients and the assessment of the treatment of patients are a collective endeavour involving patients, physicians, medical facilities and insurance companies, there must be a choice among the competing possibilities for division, subdivision and classification. Although the reality of a cancer growth is indisputable, its manifestation and progression do not correspond uniformly and perfectly to natural lines of demarcation that can be identified and classified. Human judgement about cancer, as about any other prognosis of a disease, is an integral element in the identification and description of this reality. We conclude, then, that medical categories are created as well as discovered.

As a result, one must identify particular communities of investigators or practitioners and then map out in detail the rules of evidence, inference and negotiation each community shares. A scientific or medical community sharing an explanation can be identified by its capacity to resolve a controversy by appeal to rational arguments (as when a dispute turns on epistemic issues in an unapplied science) or by its capacity to resolve a controversy by appeal to procedures for negotiating a common understanding or intervention (as when a dispute turns on non-epistemic issues in an applied science). Thus, it is unlikely that medicine as a whole shares all explanations in common. As Kuhn recognized, social structures that bind together one community of scientists may exclude other communities of scientists. They will bind together surgeons on the one hand, and general practitioners on the other, for instance, and exclude either side from easily agreeing on the merits of particular surgical versus nonsurgical approaches to the treatment of coronary artery disease. Similarly, they will set apart mental health professionals in one part of the world from another, as seen in cases of "culture bound illnesses" (Glossary of Culture Bound Syndromes 2006). Although at first "spells" (found in the southern USA), "zar" (found in Ethiopia) and "hsieh-ping" (found in Taiwan) all refer to brief trances brought about by possession, that which is possessing has different interpretations in the different cultures, from ancestral evil spirits and ancestral ghosts to diseased relatives. Different rituals and remedies have been developed to eradicate such spirits or ghosts, depending on the medical, cultural and religious norms. Although some of these culture-bound syndromes appear to have shared signs and symptoms, others do not, such as anorexia nervosa, a condition found in clinical textbooks in the developed north but unrecorded in developing countries in Africa, South America and Asia.

It is in this sense, as Galen noted, that medicine is part science and part art. And as such, it cannot claim for its practitioners the scientific models of explanation and prediction that are commonly associated with science as such. The fact that science as such is itself under intense scrutiny for its failure fully to comply with its own criteria of practice, including objectivity, value-neutrality, universality, uniformity, self-policing, correcting of mistakes and critical rationality, exacerbates the practice of medicine too. Yet it is crucial to recognize that an appreciation of the sociohistorical character of knowledge claims does not doom one to a hopeless relativity with regard to knowledge claims. Relativism, the view that there is no foundation of knowledge to which all can and must appeal and therefore anything goes, fails for conceptual and practical reasons. Conceptually speaking, relativism advances the view that "truth is relative". If the claim is taken seriously, then it backfires on itself: if it is true, it must be false. If truth is relative, then the claim itself is relative, thereby undermining its ability to establish anything. Practically speaking, relativism fails to take into account what common sense tells us: that we do act as if there is understanding or certainty in our world (for more on this, see Gifford 1983). We rely on science and medicine to explain our world, however awkwardly and partially, and they are often quite successful in doing so. When we find mistakes in our thinking or our explanations, we have ways of correcting and revising them, so as to be more accurate and successful in our attempts in the future. We have a consistent and effective set of language to describe human disease, dysfunction and disformity that many agree works.

Disease is not, then, relative. Disease is a term we have for the observed signs and reported symptoms that patients bring to the attention of health care providers and researchers. Granted, it is also in the early twenty-first century a term that refers to the asymptomatically ill, especially in cases of early detection of cancers or genetic disorders. Either way, disease is an evolving notion that provides structure and significance to patient complaints and clinical reality. In talking about disease, then, one must identify the particular community of clinicians and scientists to which one makes reference. Are we talking about "psychosis" in the west, "zar" in Ethiopia or "hseih-ping" in Taiwan? Each community is defined by its own rules of evidence, inference and ways of negotiating disagreement. Clinicians and scientists and informed patients who are members of a particular community know which facts are important and why. They know when particular facts warrant particular conclusions. In medicine, these conclusions often serve as grounds for treatment warrants or intervention that incorporate implicit, if not explicit, value judgements about proper trade-offs between costs and benefits, or harms and goods. Where a psychiatrist may recommend pharmaceuticals for psychosis, a shaman might advise the suffering individual to increase his devotion to his creator/Creator. The character of proper trade-offs will often be negotiated without a claim that the correct answers can be discovered. Disease is in part a negotiated reality (Cutter 2003, 2005). Despite the unavailability of absolute, unbiased knowledge and guidelines for practice, medicine is not doomed to a hopeless relativity with regard to its knowledge and treatment claims.

Contextualizing medical reality

As we have seen, and given that theories of medicine are themselves instruments of human adaptation, knowing is never purely a theoretical endeavour but a form of practice or "praxis" (Wartofsky 1976). How one conceives of the relation between theory and practice, then, is critical in the formulation of epistemologies that adequately reflect how medical claims are fashioned. First, one can understand the relation between theory and practice in terms of an interplay between knowledge and experience (e.g. Achenstein 1983). The relation here is one between object and subject, other and self. As the previous discussion of medicine indicates, this relation is not supported by our analysis because it separates object from subject, observation from interpretation and facts from values. Although modern medicine may try to adopt the distinction between object and subject, and observations and interpretation, through, for instance, a movement away from the bedside to the laboratory where supposedly only "facts" matter, it will in the end be unable to sustain them. In so far as medicine is devoted to the care and cure of patient complaints, it cannot (essentially) separate signs from symptoms and medical facts from the values held by patients, scientists and clinicians regarding the character and affect of medical phenomena.

A second way to understand the relation between theory and practice is in terms of the relation between theory and observation (e.g. Feinstein 1967, and to be discussed more fully in Chapter 3). The relation here is one of a body of universal statements (in the so-called rationalist tradition) or a systematically ordered body of data (in the so-called empiricist tradition). One will note that the terms "rationalism" and "empiricism" are in some sense arbitrary designations that attempt to classify so-called distinct (and for some essentialist) approaches to knowledge. Although there are indeed varying accounts of each, the specific formulation of which is assigned to the developer (e.g. Cartesian rationalism), rationalism tends to focus on how "reason" leads to the discovery of knowledge whereas empiricism (e.g. Humean empiricism) attends to how empirical data or observations construct knowledge. As the previous discussion indicates, this relation between rationalism and empiricism, or theory and observation, is unhelpful in our analysis because it separates reason from sense experience, discovery from invention and nature from nurture, which is not reflective of medical knowledge. This is the case because medicine places us at the crossroads, so to speak, between what is given and what is constructed, what is genetic and what is environmental, unable to distinguish essentially between such realms of existence. We recognize that we can never know what is solely genetic – and what is solely environmental – because we can "get outside" neither our genes nor our environment. Thus, conceiving theory and practice in terms of reason and empirical data fails to account adequately for medical knowledge.

There is something else going on here that leads us to reject the view that we must choose between rationalism and empiricism. Taken together, rationalism and empiricism assume that the universal features of knowledge acquisition by individuals are based on presuppositions or arguments that *all* individuals (collectively speaking) are the same, in capacity or structure. More specifically, rationalism assumes that individuals are all rational, and empiricism assumes that we all have the same sensory or perceptual capacities. Such assumptions about the universal character of knowledge are questionable. If knowledge is universal, it is asocial, or independent of sociocultural forces. But this position contradicts the very position advocated by rationalists and empiricists, who affirm a *sociality* of knowledge in so far as *all* human beings are considered to share in the universal features of reasons or sense-perception (Wartofsky 1992). Thus, again, neither rationalism nor empiricism by itself adequately accounts for medical knowledge.

A third way to understand the relation between theory and practice is a historical biological or practical epistemological one. This relation conceives knowledge as an evolving process involving the interaction between organisms and their environments. The relation here consists of a tension between passive contemplation or reception of empirical data by the knowing subject and active knowledge by actual practical activity in the world through, for example, the rational adaptation of an environment to life needs. This is the sense of theory–practice relation that Wartofsky (1992) finds most helpful for understanding medical knowledge. Rather than setting up a relation between knowledge and experience, or theory or observation, both of which are passive in the knower's relation to the known, this third way of understanding medical knowledge sets up a dynamic relation between discovery and creation, knowing and doing, and receiving and giving, which provides fertile ground for exploring knowledge not only in medicine but in other subjects as well (which we will not be tempted by here).

Our challenge, then, is to recast the relation between theory and practice in medicine in its most concrete expressions provided by specific historical contexts. The extent to which, for example, Galen provided impetus for the development or inhibition of applied medical techniques could be worked out. Instead of simply dismissing him as a clinician of the past without anything to offer except an outdated theory of health as balance among elements, one could explore how his contributions make sense not only of what is observed but also of how life is experienced and practised. No doubt clinicians eighteen hundred years ago "observed" and patients "experienced" (as we do today) variation in bodily heat and flow. A likely response to such variations is to offer ways to rebalance the bodily heat or flow through the use of hot and cold compresses and means (e.g. herbs) that encourage or deter bodily heat or flow. And that is what Galen did. Such lessons are instructive when we consider how conditions today, such as menopause, are understood and manipulated. What are our assumptions about menopause and about ageing women? Why is menopause a source of attention in medicine at all? How is menopause currently treated, and on what assumptions are these treatments defended? To quote Wartofsky, there are "rich, historical contexts of fundamental and even revolutionary modes of cognitive praxis" (1976: 188) that await investigation.

The clinical epistemology offered here, then, finds affinity with a contextual account of knowledge. A contextual account of knowledge denies the existence of basic statements in the foundationalist's sense and it denies that coherence as it has traditionally been explained (through metaphors depicting proper fit) is insufficient for justification. Both foundationalist (Chisholm 2003) and coherence (Dancy 1985) accounts of knowledge overlook contextual parameters necessary for justifications. In particular, and according to Annis (1978), they overlook the "issue-context" and the social nature of knowledge and its justification. The "issue-context" determines the level of understanding and knowledge that the knower and appropriate objector group must exhibit. For instance, in the context of medical diagnosis, the gold standard, if you will, will be not non-medically trained persons but qualified medical examiners. In the context of the medical diagnosis of AIDS, the gold standard would be most likely to come from a group of infectious disease specialists and not a group of gerontologists. Since the issue-context is embedded in a social nexus, the beliefs, information and theories of others are an important part in the process of justification, because they help to determine what objections will be raised, how a knower will respond to them and what responses the objectors will accept. One begins to see why infectious disease specialists reacted so strongly against the South African Minister of Health at the Thirteenth International AIDS Conference in Durban, South Africa, when he asserted that "poverty, not HIV, causes AIDS" (National Public Radio 24 July 2000). For the critics, the biological data provided the basis for justification of the position they held; for public policy representatives, socioeconomic conditions matter. If this account is correct, then, justification and its objections will be primarily "local" as opposed to global in character (Annis 1978; Longino 1997; Cutter 2003: Ch. 8).

A contextual or local account of knowledge is to be distinguished from a "naturalized" or relativist one. Although this point has already been made, it is worth emphasizing once again. First, it distinguishes itself from a "naturalized epistemology" (Antony 2002), one that holds that objective, impartial, natural and universal standards of behaviour are reducible to empirical data, such as what is produced in and by science. In that this view reduces reality to facts, thereby delinking facts from values, it cannot guide us in thinking through clinical cases. Clinical cases invariably involve a set of values, including cost–benefit ones (e.g. which treatment is better for the patient), moral concerns (e.g. whether the patient consents to the recommended treatment) and cultural commitments (e.g. whether the individual as a member of a particular culture sees the medical intervention as in keeping with his or her cultural mores).

A localized epistemology also distinguishes itself from a "relativist" one. The relativist view, as we understand it, suggests that what we call epistemology is really ideology, that there is no such thing as a foundation for knowledge and that the word "knowledge" is simply another term for the arbitrary pronouncements of whoever happens to be in power. In the end, all is arbitrary and chaotic, a view that we have already shown to be problematic and not relevant to medicine. In that relativism delinks ideas, concepts and values from historical and epistemological contexts (thereby engaging in the same essentialist thinking as the naturalist), it cannot guide us in thinking about clinical issues. As we have shown, clinical knowledge, albeit diverse and complex, is not and cannot be ahistorical and oblivious to sociocultural concerns.

The challenge, then, is this: if one affirms the importance of context and rejects a single foundation of knowledge, what basis does one have for resolving competing claims to truth or moral standard? Here we might turn to Karl Popper (1966; see Sassower 2006) for general guidance. Like Fleck, Popper is talking about major issues in twentieth-century thought well before others make them popular. Through his account of "situational logic", Popper provides what can be loosely termed as a version of social epistemology, a concern with the view of the production and dissemination of knowledge through a network of institutional agencies, all of which are dynamically involved in the evaluation and consumption of a variety of forms of knowledge. In navigating the waters between hard-core empiricism as a form of naturalism and relativism, Popper offers an account of knowledge that validates scientific judgements in situation-specific circumstances so that judgements of empirical evidence may be made. Such judgements are not simply reducible to psychological or ethical accounts (which are then vulnerable to being solely individualistic or a product of personal pleas). As he says,

The method of applying a situational logic to the social sciences is not based on any psychological assumptions concerning the rationality (or otherwise) of "human nature." On the contrary: when we speak of "rational behavior" or of "irrational behavior" then we mean behavior which is, or is not, in accordance with the logic of that situation. In fact, the psychological analysis of an action in terms of its (rational or irrational) motive presupposes – as has been pointed out by Max Weber – that we have previously developed some standard of what is to be considered as rational in the situation in question.   (Popper 1966: 97)

Here "logic" and "rational" refer to a process of intersubjectivity, because it is too much to expect objectivity in the traditional sense. This refers to a sense of a logical reconstruction and of purposiveness in the light of what is being reconstructed within the context of particular communities.

As an extension of Popper's insight, consider how we already take for granted different levels of justification for knowledge claims and the importance of context. It does not come as a surprise to us that the truth conditions of sentences of the form "S knows that P" and "S does not know that P" vary in certain ways according to the contexts in which the sentences are uttered (DeRose 1992). Revising a case from Annis (1978), suppose we are interested in whether Smith, a non-medical person, knows that AIDS is caused by HIV. If he responds that a pamphlet that he recently picked up at his local health fair states that it does, then we would say that Smith knows that HIV causes AIDS. He has performed adequately given the context. But suppose the context is an examination for an MD degree (with a specialization in infectious disease). Here we expect a lot more. If the candidate simply says what Smith said, we would say that the candidate does not know what causes AIDS because HIV infection involves more than the virus; it involves a vulnerable host, cells with certain receptors that HIV finds easy to lock on to and so on. Things become trickier when we are considering the response that the public health minister gave at the 2000 AIDS conference in South Africa that "poverty, and not HIV, causes AIDS". Although his claim received international attention and outcries from infectious disease specialists, the minister is in some sense correct when it comes to the greater context of AIDS: that HIV leads to AIDS in citizens of the poorest regions in Africa and that the appropriate response to AIDS is not pharmaceuticals but political and economic initiatives that target poverty and the social conditions of a people. Yet, if this public health official were to answer on an infectious disease examination that poverty causes AIDS, the medical examiners could claim that his answer was false based on the context in which the claim is made.

To review, a person may be justified in knowing P but not justified in knowing P relative to the context. The context determines the level of understanding and knowledge that S must exhibit, and it determines what Annis calls the appropriate "objector-group". In the context of the examination for an MD degree, the appropriate group is not the class of ordinary non-medical personnel, but qualified medical examiners. Since the context is embedded in a social nexus, the beliefs, information and theories of others are an important part of the justification that a certain claim is "true" because they in part determine what objections will be raised, how a knower will respond to them and what responses the objectors will accept. It is in this way that one can affirm the importance of context yet reject the view that knowledge has a single foundation.

A brief look at the concept of the "gene" provides an additional example of what a Popperian rational reconstruction might look like and how helpful it is to clarify the concepts that are being used in a discussion, in this case one involving genetic health and disease. The concept of the gene plays a major role in contemporary medicine, but it is anything but simple. As Petter Portin (2002) tells us, the term "gene" was coined by Wilhelm Johanssen (1909: 143–4) and has undergone a change in medicine since its inception. Portin suggests that we think of the change in the concept of the gene in terms of three distinct historical periods of thought. A first period is the *classical view* (early 1910 to the 1930s) (Mendel

1866), in which the gene is widely regarded as an indivisible unit of genetic transmission, recombination, mutation and function. The action of one gene (supposedly) leads to one enzyme, and so on. A second period is the *neoclassical view* (late 1940s to the early 1970s) (Avery *et al*. 1944; Watson and Crick 1953), in which the gene is a cistron, or stretch of DNA made up of contiguous nucleotides that code for a single messenger RNA and thus indirectly for a single polypeptide or building block of protein. Here the action of one cistron leads to one polypeptide. A third period may be referred to as the *modern period* (late 1970s to the present) (for overview, see Portin 2002), in which the gene is a unit of transmission that may be understood using the tools of evolutionary biology. It is a place-holder of sorts for a dynamic process of historical inheritance, which takes place within dynamic environments. As Portin says, "The complete DNA sequence of an organism, its genotype, is a concrete entity, but the genotype determines the norm of reaction, which for its part, is an abstract concept. It is the total whole of the *possibilities* residing in the genes" (*ibid.*: 275). Given this mosaic of interpretations, it is important to ask ourselves what we mean when we use the term "gene" prior to advancing an analysis of genetic health and disease. It is likely that those participating in the discussion will bring varying interpretations to bear, ones that reflect the particular communities (e.g. Dawkins's "genic selection-ists", population biologists) in which they operate.

Consider some of the views of the gene that we hear about today and note their indebtedness to past accounts. The classical view of the gene as an indivisible unit is expressed in the saying "the gene for". All one has to do is pick up a magazine to read how scientists are investigating the gene "for" this and the gene "for" that. All one has to do, then, is engineer that gene and a cure results. Too bad that it is not this simple. Even so-called single gene disorders such as cystic fibrosis and sickle cell anaemia are more complex than previously thought. Similarly, the view that "it's *in* the genes" is misleading. Units of DNA do not work in isolation from each other but are part of a larger system of biochemical interactions. The modern view of the gene leads us to reject essentialist and reductionist thinking. To understand a "gene", then, one must specify what biochemical processes are associated with what kind of phenotypical expression set within what particular environment. The task of specifying all the variables can be daunting, but is required in order to understand the complexity and variations in genetic expression. It will be additionally important in developing safe and effective genetic therapies. Medical knowledge and practice are in this sense contextual.

The point is that a rational reconstruction of how we understand and treat in medicine clarifies what we know from what we do not know, sets our claims in their appropriate historical contexts and highlights what problems call out for attention. It is in this sense that it is contextual knowledge.

Knowing and valuing

In so far as medical knowledge is not simply for knowledge's sake but for the sake of action, medical knowledge is evaluative (Engelhardt 1996). It involves making judgements regarding what conditions are worth reporting to health care professionals, what conditions should be investigated and what conditions ought to be treated. The values that frame disease – and that are inseparable from medical theories, facts and practices – are evident and varied.

To begin with, disease involves dysfunction, disability or impairment, often evaluated in terms of the function of an organ, tissue, cell and now gene. Since the single assessment of the activity or structure of an organ (e.g. heart), tissue (e.g. cervical), cell (e.g. pancreatic cell) or gene (e.g. BRCA-1) is highly uninformative by itself, a clinician has no idea from just one single case what range of data can count as "normal" and what range can count as "abnormal" for this particular case. Group data are accumulated and variations among subjects are considered. What is needed is a range of data from a range of populations that are considered "diseased" or "healthy" (Feinstein 1967). In other words, disease is understood in terms of a *range* of measurements that deviate from what is more "typical" for members of a group of similar characteristics (e.g. age, sex). The determination of what is *functional* is evaluative, in that judgements are made regarding what is typical versus atypical for a large population and therefore remain only a heuristic for any single patient.

Judging the difference between what is "typical" versus "atypical", or "normal" and "abnormal", is more than a fact-based determination. The terms themselves are ambiguous. As Murphy (1976: 117–33) indicates, normal may mean (a) statistical, (b) average or mean, (c) typical or expectable, (d) conducive to survival of the species, (e) innocuous or harmless, (f) commonly aspired to and (g) most perfect or excellent in its class. In the case of a normal female, for instance, she (a) is XX, (b) has pain related to her periods, (c) will have an offspring, (d) can reproduce, (e) will reach menopause by age 60, (f) wants to be safe and (g) is "36, 24, 36" in the American fashion industry. The very choice to select certain phenomena for investigation as normal or abnormal involves evaluation – one set of phenomena are considered worthy of attention over another. Typically in medicine, what is selected as calling for a response is a phenomenon that is unwanted; it is a source of pain and suffering for a patient who seeks its elimination or alleviation.

The search for particular means for the elimination or alleviation of the patient's complaints involves *instrumental* values as well. What biological pathways are explored and what treatments are attempted will depend on what explorations are possible (given current theoretical frameworks) and practical (given technological capacities). Certain goals will be established concerning what benefits are desired by the patient (e.g. feeling good, looking good, reducing pain) as well as the health care professional (e.g. helping the patient, notoriety, making money) and what harms need to be avoided (e.g. premature death of a patient, bankruptcy). In classifying cancer, for example, clinicians are concerned to minimize transaction (e.g. financial) and opportunity (e.g. morbidity and mortality) costs to the patient and related party. Recall the example given on page 55 on the need to revise the Pap smear classification to ensure that squamous cell carcinoma in women is detected at its earliest stage. If one adopts standards that are too lax, one may unduly increase the financial, social and personal costs for the care of individuals as well as society at large. However, if one sets the standards for treatment too strictly, one will pay the costs in the loss of lives. As a consequence, clinicians along with patients will want to decide a prudent balancing of the transaction and opportunity costs relating to over- and undertreating. Such an assessment requires a prior one involving the comparative significance of the possible benefits and harms involved in the possible choices.

Along with instrumental values, *aesthetic* values frame our understanding of disease (Khushf 1999). Aesthetic values enter into how we understand disease in the sense that ideal states of anatomical, physiological and psychological function presume a level of human form, movement or grace. Such values are to be distinguished from instrumental ones in that form and function are here considered "beautiful" or "ugly" as opposed to "beneficial" or "harmful". Consider karposi sarcoma, which appears in cases of AIDS. Karposi sarcoma is not only harmful in that it disrupts cellular function, it is ugly. Discoloured and irregular blotches on the body where they typically do not appear are not aesthetically pleasing in developed countries with great emphasis on youth, certain physical form and cleanliness. As humans, we typically seek what is beautiful by design and order in our world; it is no different in medicine.

Finally, how one understands disease involves choices. The choice to pay attention to a patients' complaint, the choice to fund, the choice to treat and the choice to accept a certain ranking of benefits over burdens when treating involve decisions on the part of the observer. These choices are not simply instrumental or aesthetic, but *moral* or *ethical* as well. Who gets to assign and weigh the values at stake? Who is "the" or "an" authority and why? Who is responsible for the decisions that are made and how? In cases involving patient complaints, what *ought* to be or *should* be done and why? How ought health care be structured and who pays for what? Although the next chapter still surveys and critically engages epistemological issues, we would like to emphasize at this juncture how these issues turn out to be intimately connected and bring to the forefront ethical issues involving rights, welfare and justice, a topic that receives additional attention in Chapter 4.

In closing, there are good reasons to rethink what and how we know in medicine. We have found that medicine operates with a plurality of epistemologies in understanding and intervening in the clinical setting. These epistemologies are not simply a function of select cognitive criteria but involve a host of considerations involving practical, evaluative, social, cultural, economic and political ones. All of this is to recognize the contextual character of medicine and the special challenges that face us. The more one recognizes these conditions, the more medicine will enhance human goals and offer care for patients that is appropriate and responsible.

3

Medical certainty revisited

As we have illustrated in Chapter 2, epistemological questions in general have multiple answers that affect how we think about ethics and how we behave as humans. In particular, we argued that debates and controversies that are found in the medical context are in fact predicated on epistemological debates and controversies and are usually informed by rich historical backgrounds that implicitly affect those who face them. This argument was historically anchored and was replete with examples from the diagnostic arena. How are diseases classified and how are they treated? What goes into the classification of an ailment as a disease with a specified set of causes? What turns it into an entity that can be isolated from the rest of one's physical and mental health? In this chapter we plan on focusing on one particular epistemological issue – certainty – that is significant for the methods of inquiry we use and for the goals we have in mind when we launch a scientific investigation (rather than a personal exploration or quest for peace of mind).

We probably should be clear that our approach here is deliberately limited to what some call an immanent critique of the scientific approach to medicine. By immanent critique, as some in the

Frankfurt School have called it, we mean a critique internal to the workings of the field, rather than a critique that would reach out to the spiritual or the transcendent elements or features of human existence. So, when a patient is evaluated and we suggest that we cannot predict with certainty what outcome to expect, we are not alluding here to how the power of prayer, for example, can or cannot enhance the efficacy of the immune system. Is there something to this approach? Can this approach fruitfully supplement what data clinicians gather? Of course there is something to this (as Chopra 2003 and Weil 2004 suggest). But when we expose the limits of scientific certainty, we do so in order to bolster the claims that can be made with technoscientific prowess: it is the self-consciousness of the clinician that serves patients best! Here one could cite the recent works of Jerome Groopman (2007) and Atul Gawande (2007), who report on their own experiences in the clinical setting: we can do better, even with our limitations. We need to employ more critical feedback loops in order to improve the outcomes of our procedures. Our limitations can be a source of reflection and a rallying cry for improvement.

The scientific status of medicine

One of the preoccupations of philosophers of science in the past century has been the demarcation between science and non-science, whether one speaks of metaphysics or pseudo-science (e.g. Popper 1976: 41–4). These philosophers hold that certain criteria must be fulfilled to warrant calling a given body of knowledge science. Various criteria of demarcation have been proposed since the beginning of the twentieth century. The criterion of empirical testability has been agreed upon both by the logical positivists within the Vienna Circle who demanded verification and by Karl Popper who demanded falsification (1959: §§ 4, 34, 35, 37–9). According to this philosophical programme, it is crucial to distinguish between scientific inquiries and all others, for only the former allow us to progress in our attainment of scientific knowledge, namely knowledge that is certain at least in probabilistic terms (e.g. Hempel 1965). This is not to say, as the logical positivists claimed and as we have seen already in Chapter 1, that all other knowledge claims are meaningless, but to admit that all other knowledge claims are tentative and possibly mistaken (Ayer 1952). Since knowledge as such has become over the years scientific knowledge in the sense of applying more rigorous methods of inquiry and analysis (still based on what we call common sense), one could wonder if all knowledge claims have been transformed as well. That is, one could see a general transformation of knowledge into greater precision of data collection and presentation, yet observe that a great deal of our knowledge remains vague and open-ended and as such defies the precision science demands. Besides, how would one discover whether these knowledge claims are mistaken or not?

The major demand for any knowledge claim to be worthy of discussion was, and for some still is, that it be testable. This is true regardless of the area of study, be it the physical or the biological sciences. Testability, then, is considered by many as one of the most important hallmarks of putative scientific status. More precisely, this means that any knowledge claim that one wishes to add to the body of scientific knowledge must be testable at least in principle, but preferably in terms of our experience, namely that it be empirically testable (see the wonderful summary edited by Ayer 1959). What counts as empirical testing is a complicated matter, for what would be an observation according to one report, might be only a statement about someone's observation according to another (see Urmson 1956). This warning, obviously, is compounded when one deals with subjective judgements about one's pain or ailment as opposed to one's judgement about the brightness of this or that star. The situation becomes even more complicated when one takes into account the view that all observations are theory-laden, namely that there is no such thing as the "naked eye" that observes and reports what the empirical world is like (e.g. Hanson 1958, 1971).

Perhaps it would be useful to review here the genealogy of the concerns with observations, since they are supposed to be the foundation of counting something as "fact", and facts are what we collect so as to test hypotheses and theories. Facts, whether in science, law or medicine, are crucial ingredients for practice (as we make more explicit in Chapter 4). The distinction between the natural and social sciences and between them and the humanities does not fully hold when it comes to facts: in all cases there are reasons to rely on and contest facts, since all reports of facts are forwarded by humans, who are fallible in principle in so far as they are prone to make unintentional mistakes in their reporting. Their fallibility can be observed despite their best intentions and at times because of them: they are eager to confirm a theory that is well established or that is promoted by great authorities in a field of research, or they are eager to follow a trend, or they are predisposed to observing some things and overlooking others because of their own set of beliefs and values, such as the orderly revolution of the planets or the equilibrium one should discover in nature.

In this context, Gillispie reminds us, for example, that Vesalius, who taught at the University of Padua in the sixteenth century and whose image dominates textbooks on the pedagogy of medical training (the famous theatre where surgery was performed as a demonstration for medical students), remains an important milestone in medical knowledge of the time and the training of physicians. What characterized medical knowledge in the sixteenth century, according to Gillispie (1960: 60–1), was "the authority of its information, the method of exposition, and the systematic approach. . . . Vesalius's essential contribution was the comprehensive skill with which he wove them into a corpus of anatomical practice rather than originality in any single detail or method." This sentiment with regard to the slow transformation of medical knowledge based on authority to a more empirical basis is also documented in Bates's (1995) comparison of the Galenic, Chinese and Ayurvedic traditions. In short, medicine, just like the rest of the scientific enterprise and similar to the legal framework, must be careful in what is claimed as factual or universal knowledge as opposed to the knowledge handed down the generations from one group of intellectual leaders to another. This nuanced realization of the precarious status of facts and observation has a long history, and one that plays a major role, however overlooked, in discussions of disputes and puzzles regarding one's health.

In the second century, Galen worried about the collection of data, understood in his day as "experience". When discussing the empiricists, Galen notes that they rely on their perception and on their memory. Hence, their method is open to personal interpretation and multiple variations. Their "method" contributes to the "art" of healing (Galen 1985). Auguste Comte (1798–1857), the French father of positivism, recalls Bacon and claims that "there can be no real knowledge except that which rests upon observed facts". But, as he continues to explain this "fundamental maxim", he turns out to say that "every positive theory must necessarily be founded upon observations", yet that it is "no less true that, in order to observe, our mind has need of some theory or other" (Comte 1988: 4–5). Albert Einstein, as Holton (2005: 30) reminds us, maintains this sentiment as well when he says "Only the theory decides what one can observe", and thus takes direct aim at the classic Baconian sentiment of data collection. The issue here is the debate between the inductivists and the deductivists (reminiscent of the debates between the empiricists and rationalists, as Galen already noted, and as we shall observe in the history of western ideas around the sixteenth and seventeenth centuries). Is our knowledge based on the collection of observation reports that then bolster a general statement of fact that becomes a theory? Or is our knowledge based on a hypothetical conjecture (a theory, if you wish) that is being tested against the data (so as to confirm or refute it)? If our observations themselves are in need of a theoretical foundation, if they cannot be "naive" or "neutral" or "unbiased", then are we inevitably in a vicious epistemological cycle? This cycle may not be vicious in the sense of redundant or leading to an infinite regress (in a Hegelian or Nietzschean sense), but instead be informative in so far as any intervention must realize its dependence on both alternative starting points. That is, wherever you find yourself in the cycle, always remember to look backwards and forwards, noting the theoretical and the empirical components of your own choices, decisions and scientific claims.

Perhaps all that we observe is that which we expect to observe, and therefore we can never discover anything new. Perhaps our theoretical frameworks inform our observations so that they tend to confirm them and stay within predetermined paradigmatic confines. Perhaps we are trained, as scientists and doctors, to focus systematically on some important facts that could change what we think and how we treat a particular situation, and in fact do not see others. It is interesting to note here how Harvey's discovery of blood circulation was not observed prior to his own reports and how his own reports lay dormant for thirty years before they were accepted. As Gillispie documents the power of tradition and the authority of the ancients, such as Galen, on the conservatism of medical knowledge, leading to the retardation of discoveries or novel ideas, he suggests that although the Spaniard Miguel Serveto understood blood circulation from the heart to the lungs and published his observations in 1553, the western world had to await Harvey's book of 1628 to consider changing its view of blood circulation in the human body (Gillispie 1960: 66–7). Put differently, our view that observations alone would change our knowledge (part of the scientific ethos) is proven to be naive and wrong. Overturning centuries of belief is so overwhelming that the authority of our predecessors remains dominant. To some extent, Kuhn's own work (1970) is a description of this problem and in many ways serves as its modern endorsement in so far as "normal science" sets paradigms in place that are difficult to shift.

Gillispie (1960: 68–9) claims that Harvey's book remains a "classic of inductive science" and "reasoning" because of its empirical basis. Harvey is quoted here as saying: "Since calculations and visual demonstrations have confirmed all my suppositions, to wit, that the blood is passed through the lungs and the heart by the pulsation of the ventricles" (*ibid.*: 71). As Gillispie continues to explain:

> In him a new science which makes objective measurements superseded an old science which found qualities, humors, purposes, and tendencies indwelling. On yet another front, personality was displaced as a category of

scientific thinking and as the model for order. Galileo had excluded the biological metaphor from physics. Harvey went further and introduced mechanistic thinking into organic studies. And by a simple though systematic extension, Descartes would find a machine in man. Harvey's views were not generally accepted in the thirty years or more before Malpighi's discovery forced assent. As Harvey foresaw, he had against him more than force of habit. For his hydraulics of the blood stream destroyed a whole philosophy of the body in order to establish a single phenomenon of nature.   (*Ibid.*: 73)

So, here we see that four centuries ago both trained doctors and the lay public had a difficult time in changing their minds about health and disease and an even more difficult time in revising their epistemological frameworks despite empirical evidence. Nowadays this is true not only of cases, such as AIDS, where organ malfunction was keenly observed and reported, rather than a more profound underlying condition that brought about the failure of organs, but also of a host of other diseases, such as syphilis, where cultural mores and social conventions had an enormous influence on how the medical profession operated (as Fleck eloquently illustrates). Technoscience can enhance our observation potential but cannot guide its path or alert us to novel facts. Perhaps we must acknowledge that our theories have a psychological impact that turns our best "scientific" intentions of removing biases and prejudices and being objective and value-free into wishful thinking. This is not the same as the flaw of self-fulfilling predictions about which Popper (1957) speaks when discussing the "poverty of historicism". Instead, this is an ongoing appreciation in some scientific circles that observations are fraught with problems, that the observer is an active participant in the observation itself and therefore can influence the "measurement of phenomena" (Hanson 1958). What we would like to emphasize here is not that knowledge cannot be acquired or that all knowledge claims are inherently flawed and should not be trusted, but instead that there are limits to our knowledge and that it requires intellectual courage to admit to these limits and work with them. This means that at times we push ahead and at times we push back; at times we succeed in solving a puzzle and at times we get even more confused than before. This amounts to the excitement we call the adventure of the scientific enterprise. We have come a long way from the days of misguided superstition so as not to have blind faith in any absolutes, be they of the scientific or the moral kind. It is about modesty and humility in the face of a broadening horizon. Even those subscribing to the ancient "man is the measure of all things" must concede to the limitations of that measure, human or other.

What, then, counts as scientific knowledge? The criterion of empirical testability is only one of many; other traditional criteria have been proposed over the years, have been discussed at length and have been eventually criticized. Some argue that scientific knowledge must be explanatory to count as scientific (Toulmin 1961); others claim that it must be a simplified model of the world surrounding us (Hesse 1966); and still others insist that the foremost hallmark of scientific knowledge is its predictive power (Comte 1975). What counts as the set of all the criteria that must be fulfilled to make any theory scientific remains an open question. This question receives renewed answers from philosophers of science who presently rely primarily on their studies of the history of science. These philosophers examine the canonical scientific theories and try to extract a set of principles or criteria that are apparent in most of these theories (e.g. Cohen 1985).

There is, of course, a problem with this procedure that attempts to extract a set of criteria of scientific demarcation from already acknowledged scientific theories. The problem is that these studies take it for granted that Newton's theory, for example, is scientific. This acceptance can be viewed as dogmatic and in some sense begs the question of what theory should count as scientific. Other procedures seem to fare no better. If one were to set forth an *a priori* set of criteria of scientific demarcation and then begin examining the history of science for illustrations and confirming instances, one might find that no theory would qualify, or that all theories would qualify, or that some would and some would not qualify as scientific. How would we know which one of the alternatives is the correct one? There is some sort of inherent inability to substantiate any one of these alternatives exclusively without being dismissed as dogmatic by some who disagree with the findings. Any selective illustration from the history of science might continuously suffer from criticism (Agassi 1963).

Although we are not interested in providing here a definitive answer, and although this brief summary reiterates some of the quandaries already mentioned in Chapter 2, we find these issues, which are usually confined to discussions in the philosophy of science, to be relevant for our examination of medicine. For, as is apparent from the history of medicine, it is quite difficult, if not impossible, to state clearly whether or not medicine is a science (see Garrison 1929). We may find that there are many instances in which the history of medicine illustrates that certain criteria of scientific demarcation were met; by the same token, we may find that there are many instances in which medical practices ignored the standard criteria and stumbled by chance upon great discoveries and achievements (see King 1982). Since the debates over the criteria of scientific demarcation are still simmering among philosophers of science, it would be unreasonable to accept an unequivocal statement concerning the scientific status of medicine.

Lest we are misunderstood in claiming either that the questions surrounding the scientific status of medicine are unimportant or that the answers to these questions are impossible to find, let us add at once that we find these questions and their competing answers to be of the utmost importance because of their practical implications. To some extent there is here an existential quest for scientific knowledge, a way of gaining some level of certitude about one's health and the methods of its preservation. Medicine strives to be scientific for all the right reasons. We include here both medical researchers who work in laboratories or in hospitals and who follow the standard scientific methodology of the day, and physicians who administer medical care and treatment in clinical settings (public or private). Medical practitioners generally aspire to fulfill whatever criteria are established by the scientific community so as to take better care of their patients and provide a more informed procedure whenever possible. In their training, in medical schools and in hospitals, medical practitioners are taught the methodological principles and relevant data of the natural sciences so as to give their eventual medical care and treatment a scientific foundation (e.g. Harvey *et al.* 1972). So, regardless of one's judgement concerning the scientific status of medicine, we can conclude here that medical practitioners view themselves personally and existentially as scientists carrying on the scientific enterprise of medicine. This, of course, does not mean that in their practice physicians are unaware of nonscientific aspects of their care and treatment. But those are usually conceived of as additional (even if crucial) variables in their scientific equations, such as family history and lifestyle questions they ask their patients (e.g. diets and living environment), as well as their own personal belief systems that colour their own observations and medical treatment (e.g. cases of abortion for the religious physician). Obviously, there is an intimate connection between the so-called scientific and nonscientific variables, as the study of the genetics of disease illustrates, with some patients being more predisposed to certain diseases than others.

We would suggest here that the quest for scientific status has become more pronounced by the end of the twentieth century not only because of personal prestige and the accreditation of medical schools and hospitals, but also because insurance companies are more likely to reimburse physicians who are scientists than other medical practitioners who are not. The question of scientific status is, then, not simply a philosophical question or a question of epistemological demarcation (between reliable and speculative knowledge), but instead a practical question. Certainty, of course, is significant in this context, especially when decisions about life and death come up in the treatment of patients. Put differently, if the medical community wishes to affiliate itself more intimately with the scientific community in general, it must adhere not only to its general ethos (as described in Chapter 1 quoting Merton), but in some specific and easily recognizable ways, such as the precision and certainty they bring to bear on their observations and judgements.

We are less interested in the actual status of medicine, be it scientific or not, and more in the implications of the views people hold of this status as they affect the level of certainty expected from it. If medicine is scientific, and if scientific knowledge provides us with certainty, then it is reasonable to expect that medicine will provide us with certainty concerning medical matters. If we expect medicine to consist of certain knowledge, it is reasonable to expect that physicians will have no doubts concerning their practices. This expectation should hold true even when we leave some room for individual errors on the part of physicians (see Gorovitz & MacIntyre 1976).

But what if scientific knowledge itself can no longer represent itself as knowledge that is certain? Then, even if we grant medicine scientific status, we may find ourselves lowering our expectations of physicians. For we must realize that in addition to possible personal errors on the part of physicians, the whole theoretical foundations on which they base their pronouncements are uncertain too. If medicine cannot provide us with certainty concerning medical matters, in the same manner that biology cannot provide us with certainty in biological (as well as evolutionary) matters, then individual medical practitioners cannot be expected to do any better than their field as a whole. This realization has an immediate impact on the practice of medicine.

Clinical uncertainty: enrichment loops

To some extent we must realize that the scientific community has given up the naive notions of certainty – knowing for sure, having precise knowledge about specific events at specific times – and has adopted more modern notions of certainty that were developed alongside the development of the theory of probability (Todhunter 1865). Yet this changing notion of what we mean when we speak of certainty cannot be emphasized enough here, because it remains understudied by many writers on medical certainty, not to mention the general public, except, of course, statisticians in the field. They seem to pay much closer attention to the psychological aspects associated with the "quest for certainty", as John Dewey (1960) described it, than to the actual impact on science associated with the emergence and development of the theory of probability (Katz 1984b).

As Baruch Brody and Nicolas Capaldi (1968: 48–51) remind us, Werner Heisenberg suggested that unlike Newton's natural laws, whose "constants referred to the properties of things" Planck's law of radiation has a so-called constant of quantum of action that "does not describe the properties of things, but a property of Nature itself". And since "there are scales and standards in Nature", the classical descriptors of natural phenomena do not have a fixed, one-to-one reference point. When natural phenomena are described "with the concepts of classical physics", they are "determined"; but the "use of these concepts . . . is . . . limited by the so-called indeterminacy relations. These contain quantitative information concerning the limits of the use of classical concepts" (*ibid.*). The point is that even when scientific knowledge is obtained and is capable of formulating "laws" in the sense of having the explanatory and predictive power of universal assent, there are limits to their claims and even their validity. It is this sense of the limits of knowledge that must permeate any claims about medical knowledge.

This is true not only when scientists confront the messy collection of messy data. This is also true with the cleanest of endeavours, namely mathematical methods of measurement and formulations of natural laws. As Rebecca Goldstein notes in her book on Kurt Gödel (1906–78), "for Gödel mathematics is a means of unveiling the features of objective mathematical reality, just as for Einstein physics is a means of unveiling aspects of objective physical reality" (Goldstein 2005: 45). This "unveiling" sounds Platonic in some respects, since it presupposes that there is a reality already there to be unveiled. Yet it also explains the limits of human unveiling: some secrets remain hidden, some puzzles remain unsolved. The scientific enterprise, as Goldstein sees it through the eyes of

Einstein and Gödel, is exciting and surprising, almost magical. In her words:

> Far from restoring us to the center of the universe, describ-
> ing everything as relative to our experiential point of view,
> Einstein's theory, expressed in terms of beautiful mathe-
> matics, offers us a glimpse of an utterly surprising physical
> reality, surprising precisely *because* it is nothing like what
> we are presented with in our experiential apprehension of
> it. (*Ibid.*: 42)

So, despite the general view of Einstein's relativity and Gödel's incompleteness principle – the two hallmarks of contemporary science in relation to its uncertainty – Goldstein wishes to remind us that there is some objective reality, metaphysically and ontolog-ically speaking, that anchors their recognition of their own human limitations. As she says, "Gödel's metamathematical view, his affirmation of the objective, independent existence of mathematical reality, constituted perhaps the essence of his life . . . his Platonism, which was the deepest expression, therefore, of the man himself" (*ibid.*: 47–8).

Perhaps Goldstein's take on the giants of the early and middle part of twentieth-century science helps to bring the psychological elements of our discussion to a level different from simply the personal or existential one. All of this is not meant to minimize the importance of the psychological character of our notions of certainty. Instead, following Goldstein, we wish to direct our atten-tion here to some social and moral issues associated with scientific certainty, or more precisely, with the adoption of certain views of certainty as manifest in science in general and in medicine in par-ticular. If scientific status is a preferred status in contemporary society, and if this status is granted to medicine, then medicine as science may have other claims of certainty than if it were not a science. These claims of certainty, we believe, should be updated and appreciated in their present postmodern context, rather than remaining connected to outdated notions of certainty as expressed in the middle ages. The battleground of modernity has left behind the spectre of superstition with the advance of scientific knowledge and certainty. The promise was just as extreme, and as such extremely unrealistic, of knowing for sure and having a certain foundation on which knowledge claims could rest assuredly. But the promise survived the attacks of scepticism because it offered a way of explaining the past and predicting the future so that the present was more palatable. It is this postmodern context that comes into play when medicine is discussed.

In addition to the view medical practitioners have of themselves, there is also a public view of the "science" of medicine. The public seems to view medicine today as a science that provides scientific answers to medical questions, regardless of whether this cannot in principle be supported by acceptable evidence or remains mere wishful thinking. Yet it is quite reasonable (even rational, some would say) for postmodern society, which has given up magic and superstition for the sake of scientific knowledge, to have replaced its awe of witchdoctors with an awe of modern physician-scientists who can "see genes" or detect diseases with their dazzling new technologies (Gellner 1979). This replacement is well documented and is held to be the outcome of the rationalization of our daily life in the Weberian (1978) sense. Moreover, the shift in the view of nature in general and medicine in particular is interwoven with the shift to seeing the potential of human intervention, once again, in nature in general and medicine in particular. As Edward Yoxen explains from the perspective of a genetic engineer:

> The dominant image of nature in the second half of the twentieth century, deepened by the insights of genetics, is less reverential than that of the eighteenth, and places less emphasis on struggle and competition than that of the nineteenth. Nature is a system of systems. Organisms function, reproduce and evolve as systems ordered by their genes, "managed" by the programme in their DNA. Life is the processing of information. The same concepts, drawn from computer science, cryptography, programming and

control engineering, fit the design of an early warning system for intercontinental missiles, the patterns of activity in
an anthill, the use of numerically controlled machine tool,
the control of blood pressure and the way in which cells
make protein molecules.   (Yoxen 1983:15)

Yoxen documents the shift in the second half of the twentieth
century from a static view of nature to a dynamic view of the systems that compose natural phenomena. What propels these systems, according to Yoxen, is the transfer of information, so that our
understanding of nature parallels the development in computer
technology in so far as we can get a better handle of how to tran-
scribe natural changes as data transfers and how these transfers are
in fact transmissions of information. It is in this sense, then, that
Yoxen claims that "we are now at the stage where merely thinking of
organisms as programmed systems is giving way to the activity
of reprogramming them" (*ibid.*). And as we become active participants in these processes as opposed to observers who record what
is happening in nature, "our image of nature is coming more and
more to emphasize human intervention through a process of
design. More and more, genes, organisms, biochemical pathways
and industrial bioreactors and processes can be realized according
to a prior specification. Now, the essence of life is its constructabil-
ity" (*ibid.*) So, we may conclude with Yoxen that the view medicine
has of its own scientific status with regard to its genetic composition and potential intervention is reinforced by the public that sees
in this epistemological transformation a way of ensuring better
health, more rapid intervention to cure diseases and prevent defor-
mities, not to mention a sure way of apprehending with certainty
how our organisms and organs operate.

The nature of medical certainty, whether at the genetic level
or any other level of study, may vary within clinical practice. The
degree to which certainty is sought may change over time and
within different medical settings. One can envision, as Eric Juengst
(1995, 1998) does, that degrees of certainty can be assigned to
different aspects and procedures in medical treatment akin to the

differentiation we commonly accept in the legal context: from probable cause and circumstantial evidence to evidence or eye-witness testimony that is beyond the shadow of the doubt. The language of certainty may depend on whether one is focusing on the classical categories of medical diagnosis, therapy or prognosis, which are themselves, as we shall see below, problematic. While our discussion of scientific certainty does not categorize areas of medical practice as more or less scientific, and thus demanding a specific level of certainty, one could suggest that society and physicians generally expect greater diagnostic and therapeutic certainty, while appreciating some limitations on prediction for future prognostic outcomes. There is a sense that whereas prognosis is a value-laden prediction, diagnosis is an empirical factual judgement based on past experiences (except in cases when doubt permeates). Neither is the case, yet some implications for the exploration of the relationship of certainty to responsibility are critical. Diagnosis, treatment and prognosis are at once both intimately related and independently derived. Whether a physician "knows" the diagnosis, applies the "appropriate" therapy or achieves the "optimal" outcome, the patient as a "closed system" will have manifested all of these elements as a unique unit. Yet each component of this system may be addressed, perceived and defined independently as well. Likewise, each component is dependent on the others and is intimately affected by them as well.

Before we continue to assess the different aspects of the medical enterprise, we wish to acknowledge that the very distinction of diagnosis, treatment and prognosis might be flawed. There is a sense in which all three categories are interconnected and cannot be easily separated, so that when we do so at this stage of our argument, this is more for convenience's sake and for the sake of trying to explore the possibility of detecting different levels and layers of certainty to be associated with medical practice. Now that on the theoretical level of science we have realized our limitations and our inability to claim certainty, there is no reason not to appreciate this at the practical, clinical and bioethical levels (more on this in Chapter 4). As we shall see in what follows, medical treatment can itself be understood as empirical testing, since we can then appreciate successes and failures in treatments and collect data so as to rethink our approach to this or that disease. More generally, the three categories of diagnosis, treatment and prognosis provide an information loop or cycle that keeps on transforming its individual components. That is, from the moment a patient complains about an ailment, that ailment is classified and tested against other such reports, and the patient's treatment is monitored along the way to observe any normal or abnormal results (in the sense of therapeutic efficacy), so that data are gathered with regard to the said diagnosis. The treatment itself is then evaluated in comparison to the diagnosis so that the diagnosis itself can be revised, if needed, or maintained, if the results prove successful. Obviously, the diagnosis becomes a moving target in the light of the results of the therapies or treatments and as such could inform the clinicians about the accuracy of the original diagnosis. At times, the treatment is a direct test of the diagnosis, at times it is a "best guess" when diagnosis is too vague or noncommittal. Likewise, the prognosis that is suggested at any given point is itself open to revisions because the treatment may or may not be successful. To stop at one point is to break the cycle and thereby postulate an incomplete and even arbitrary perspective. Despite the disclaimer here, or perhaps because of it, we nonetheless proceed with the three categories as separate areas only to link them at the end.

(a) One can define diagnosis as the point in time when we determine the nature of the disease. The diagnosis and questions surrounding the certainty of that pronouncement is usually the point of entry of the patient into the medical system. Within a medical model, patients come to physicians with a constellation of subjective symptoms/complaints (an illness), which are subsequently converted to signs and an objective "scientific" diagnosis (a disease) so that an "appropriate" medical therapy might be sought to cure the patient's disease. Within this framework, a patient should have a definitive or "close to certain" diagnosis prior to embarking on medical therapies. Finally, without a diagnosis and subsequent adequate therapy, one cannot approach certainty with regard to outcome or prognosis. This is so because the treatment and prognosis are so intimately tied to proper diagnosis. The case of genetic therapy in the western world comes to mind as a case study for this classification (see Juengst 1998).

Why does medicine strive for diagnostic certainty? A simple answer might be that this is what the patient has contracted/come to the medical profession for. Knowledge of diagnosis from the patient's standpoint, however, may be of an instrumental nature (to know for a purpose or an end); medicine, on the other hand, may search for such knowledge so that a disease might be named or characterized and that labelling would become uniform, verifiable and consistent. The predictive implications of the search for a diagnosis may also spur clinicians to diagnostic certainty. If medicine is a science, and if inductive reasoning is employed, then the diagnosis and subsequent events might be intimately tied to theories, notions of causality and specific conceptualizations of the physical world. By contrast, if deductive reasoning is employed, then any diagnosis is a hypothesis waiting to be empirically tested.

One outgrowth of medicine's need for, and striving to, diagnostic certainty is its preoccupation with the use of technoscience as a means for achieving more certain knowledge about a patient's condition. The advent of laboratory tests on all body fluids, the use of X-rays and scanners, and probes of all sorts are testimony to this quest for greater certainty. In some instances, the technology has actually taken on a "life of its own", where the goals of medical encounter focus on technology in determining patient care as opposed to patient care determining the extent of technological intervention. Although there is a danger in the science of medicine becoming a goal in itself, the justification for technology has generally been directed towards the concept of diagnostic certainty – being related to better patient care and thus presumably better therapy and prognosis.

For example, the case of pre-eclampsia, which is "a poorly understood disorder that affects five percent of pregnant women" and which "is one of the leading causes of maternal death", is useful to examine in this context not only because "it is thought to kill more than seventy-five thousand women each year in the United States alone" (Groopman 2006: 26), but because it remains a mysterious pregnancy disorder. "The only cure is delivery", according to physicians interviewed by Groopman (*ibid.*). The underlying causes of the disorder have not been studied, so no definite causal connection, genetic or otherwise, has been established. Although diagnosis remains tied to high blood pressure, and although treatment as such is minimal (except in cases when pre-eclampsia appears at the early stages of pregnancy), treatment is quite clear: delivery cures. Although there is a degree of clinical certainty based on past experiences, there is an underlying degree of medical uncertainty with regard to the root causes of the disorder and the therapeutic manner in which intervention at early stages of pregnancy can be effective. Benjamin Sachs, the chief of obstetrics and gynaecology at Beth Israel Deaconess hospital in Boston, calls the disorder "the disease of theories" (Groopman 2006: 27), because no conclusive, unifactorial explanation is available at this point. Reliance on more precise experimental studies would enhance the knowledge of what causes the disorder and provide greater certainty as to what is in fact being diagnosed and eventually treated.

Several other reasons exist for the use of technology in an attempt to reach diagnostic certainty. Many physicians who become investigators with pharmaceutical or public funding, for example, are challenged by the intellectual and scientific pursuit of truth. The diagnosis becomes the validation of the hypothesis or theory constructed to explain a physical or medical phenomenon. In this sense, physicians may continue to search for the primary site of a malignancy even when the patient has such metastatic disease as to preclude any potential therapeutic endeavours to control or cure the cancer. Other reasons for focusing on diagnosis include an assumption that a better diagnostic capability will lead to a better treatment or at least to a more definitive causal connection between diagnosis and treatment. Diagnostic certainty can allow for better empirical research both retrospectively and prospectively, as well as the use of broader medical historical controls. More "accurate" diagnoses may also allow for better communication between physicians and patients with regard to treatment and prognosis, and will also aid in interphysician communication regarding the specific details of a case. Diagnostic certainty has implications for issues of negligence and accountability. The advent of diagnostic related groups (DRGs), health insurance and reimbursement has been intimately tied to diagnosis. Finally, diagnosis is the primary mechanism for linking medical care to broader public policy debates regarding health care issues, from smoking and obesity to pollution and genetic engineering.

Degrees of certainty with respect to diagnosis are also a function of the type of disease process in question. For example, a patient with a painful swollen toe may have the problem localized to a specific anatomic location. This will invite an X-ray of the toe, which will provide the basis for a specific diagnosis of a fracture associated with great certainty. On the other hand, the painful swollen toe may be the result of a more systematic physiologic imbalance of uric acid metabolism resulting in a gouty attack. The aetiology and pathophysiology may be still more obscure, with a diagnosis based on multiple organ system abnormalities and diffuse physical findings. A patient with fever, nausea, vomiting, diarrhoea, joint pain and shaky chills may have a diagnosis of flu made, but the degree of certainty will be much less and the approach to specifying a diagnosis even more obscure.

Much of what has been discussed thus far with respect to diagnostic certainty also assumes that empiricism and technological innovations will in fact lead to more definitive diagnoses. However, the problem may be that we are neither knowledgeable enough to make definite diagnoses nor capable of developing the proper tools to allow us to improve these diagnoses. Instead, diagnostic problems may depend on questionable assumptions regarding diagnostic certainty and patient care. Diagnosis may be rendered problematic by the context of medical provision. The manifestation of signs and symptoms of the disease may be developed over time and space in such a manner that certainty may be no more than a complication of interrelated observations and as such remains uncertain. Whether these medical observations are causally related and bring forth one diagnosis or are actually illustrations of added diagnoses that are independent of pre-existing ones remains an open question.

Value judgements may also preclude greater certainty with regard to the diagnosis of particular patients. The collection of patients' signs and symptoms, the compilation and collation of physical and laboratory findings, and the ultimate comparison to known medical databases are not value-free endeavours. Preconceived notions of clinical conditions, experiences with findings over time and within one practice, will all affect the way in which physicians arrive at a diagnosis. For example, obesity has become a medical problem in recent years in the United States. As Robin Marantz Henig reports, there are various studies and theories about why people are fat: "It's clear that diet and genes contribute to how fat you are. But a new wave of research suggests that, for some people, there might be a third factor: microorganisms" (Henig 2006: 28). Without going into great detail here, we would like to point out that, according to the researchers interviewed by Henig, the microbes that infest our guts find certain environments more "hospitable" than others and therefore thrive in them more readily and therefore are more likely to extract calories from foodstuff and convert them into fat (*ibid.*: 31). In short, as Henig concludes, "You might think a microbial theory of obesity could change people's views about the obese, perhaps even lessen the degree to which people think that obesity is the fat person's own fault. But anti-fat sentiments seem to be deeply ingrained and resistant to change" (*ibid.*: 32).

Here we have new theories and experiments attempting to debunk one sentiment or attitude towards fat people (however we measure the category of fat or obese), while they are sceptically viewed by those wishing to assign guilt to those who happen to be overweight. Moreover, inappropriately assumed shared values between physicians and patients in a multicultural and multiethnic context might lead to disparities in some of their respective claims. What might seem a reasonable attitude or outlook about weight or about pain or about one's lifestyle may turn out to be not so for someone else. Expectations play a vital role in assessing at what cost a patient wishes to seek a diagnosis that is certain. How many tests should be conducted? How invasive should these tests be? What should be done with incompatible tests? This cost may be financial, physical, social, or psychological. Finally, health care providers might assume that a diagnosis implies knowledge of or provides licence for prescribing therapies or prognoses that are intimately related to patients' goals and values.

Diagnostic uncertainty will thus vary over time and as a function of value judgements, as well as vary over settings. The urgency with which data are collected, verified and applied is quite different in an intensive care unit than in a primary care practitioner's office. The need for and expectation of certainty will set different standards within different clinical settings; expectations concerning the degree of certainty within hospitals may vary from those in clinics and from those in hospices. Obviously, predictability of any set of conditions is problematic, since one cannot have a fully fledged explanatory model of any disease that in turn could be used as a model for prediction. As philosophers of science agreed in the twentieth century, explanatory and predictive models have the same logical structure and they all depend on a set of empirical data that establish their credibility (e.g. Toulmin 1961).

(b) We define treatment or therapy as intervention into the disease process for the purposes of alleviating, if not eliminating, patient complaints. As physicians move from diagnosis to treatment, the ability to assess certainty and the expectations for certainty may diminish. Patients seek or demand the same, if not a greater, level of certainty with respect to therapy as they do with respect to diagnosis. Therapy is often influenced by patients' wishes and thus obscures a simple discussion concerning levels of certainty that are expected (as mentioned before). Physicians also realize that although two patients may have a similar diagnosis with a high degree of certainty and thus be treated in the identical manner, this does not ensure a uniform response because there are individual variations in therapeutic responses, leading to a much lower degree of certainty, thereby rendering a precise exposition virtually impossible. For example, radiation or chemotherapy may have different results in males and females, just as they may have different results with obese patients as compared to physically fit ones.

This realization has historical antecedents, as we have seen in the case of seventeenth-century English medicine (Wear 1995: 163), where the disease was not the exclusive focus of treatment but the whole person. This alerts physicians to the need to distinguish one treatment from another, depending on the individual patient, while using all the theoretical and empirical data available from the generalizations of previous cases and treatments. The use of treatment as an empirical tool of data collection is quite obvious. Yet this tool also becomes a mode of empirical testing of diagnostic hypotheses for physicians who are uncertain about what disease afflicts a patient. Treatment as testing has the obvious disadvantage, already mentioned in Chapter 1 in relation to the Nuremberg Code, of being open to abuses. Would one treat only in order to test a hypothesis, to find out if this or that drug does or does not work? Would someone's additional suffering, however unintentional, be worth the knowledge gained from it? Here is where the rules of the IRBs come into play in the form of risk assessment when treating human subjects in an experiment. Knowledge is gained through the process, but because there is an inherent uncertainty of clinical outcomes, one may wish to be very cautious.

As we try to illustrate here, there are conditions that we can treat but do not fully understand (e.g. glaucoma), and conditions that we understand but cannot treat (e.g. we now know a lot more about Huntington's disease but cannot treat it). Prognosis will vary depending on whether we are talking about prognosis without treatment (then, our level of certainty is raised if we can diagnose), or prognosis with treatment (then our level of certainty is raised if we can treat). Increased certainty at one level helps us to navigate the search for greater certainty at another level. The more we got to know about HIV, the better we were about offering therapies that helped AIDS patients (as we currently witness in the United States). Of course, it has been difficult to understand HIV because of its mutational character, which, incidentally, is the norm and not the exception in medicine, as Myer and others argue.

(c) We define prognosis as the forecast of the disease process, which is ambiguous in so far as it can include or exclude the treatment that may ensue. When physicians move from treatment to prognosis (predicting future outcomes), certainty is always challenged. There are times when we do not understand a clinical phenomenon but are able to predict its clinical path and help the patient (e.g. the cold virus). Prognostic uncertainty may be of less concern to physicians whose initial focus is on diagnostic certainty, but is the primary concern of patients. There are value judgements inherent in predicting not only what constitutes an outcome but also what constitutes the "good" outcome or prognosis, and being unable to control exogenous factors that will influence it. If there is any sense of greater or lesser certainty associated with the various functions and operations of medicine, then we can say that prognostic certainty is at the lowest level or end of the spectrum. This also implies that the lower level of certainty already found in diagnosis, the lower the expected levels of certainty should be assigned to therapy and prognosis. So, when physicians or other health care providers claim ignorance or are at a loss as to what to say to patients and their families, they really mean it! For example, some surgical procedures in infants may allow speedy recovery in some while causing permanent damage in others.

We would be remiss if we did not interject, even if briefly, the parallel models of clinical medicine practised in parts of Asia, sometimes called eastern remedies. To some extent, the whole process of diagnosis, treatment and prognosis may seem more like the kind of religious or spiritual and in some cases supernatural frameworks already mentioned in Chapter 2. The cosmic explanation of the imbalance in one's body may bring about a suggestion for herbal therapy that seems ludicrous from a western perspective. This is not to say that Chinese medicine, for instance, has no scientific tools with which to approach medical ailments; instead, the language and models used in Chinese medicine may not conform to or seem aligned with those of the medical models taught in western medical schools and funded by pharmaceutical companies. They have explanations and predictions just like us, they have specific processes for intervention and they have collected, just like us, empirical data with which to confirm or falsify their conjectures about the causes of a disease. Perhaps their understanding of the immune system is different from ours, but that in itself should not be the decisive criterion for dismissal. Put differently, the obvious incommensurability among competing medical models need not give rise to the preference of one model over the other in some theoretical sense; instead it should be cast in some practical sense of that which works best. As Paul Feyerabend reports of his own pain and its treatment by Chinese medicine, there is a pragmatic element that overrides any and all alleged scientific models: if it works, then it is true. Besides, as he says, "pluralism of theories and metaphysical view is not only important for methodology, it is also an essential part of a humanitarian outlook" (Feyerabend 1975: 50–2).

Working with clinical uncertainty

As we have seen in the previous section, there is an epistemological and practical loop that encircles the diagnosis, treatment and prognosis of disease. We become informed from one stage to another, recalling that which has been successful or failed to bring about anticipated outcomes. We collect our data all along so that at each given moment we refer to our ongoing quest for greater knowledge base and more accuracy and efficacy in treating patients. Even when a diagnosis is "true" or "correct" in some clinical sense, it remains epistemologically problematic. Have we simply correctly noted a disease or, since we are dealing with a whole organic system, have we been able to explain its underlying causes and its epidemiological origins? Do we know for sure at this particular, arbitrary moment of diagnostic intervention what has led this patient to suffer this pain, and at what developmental level is the disease observed? Is this cancer as opposed to another expressing itself because of a genetic predisposition or because the patient has been smoking for ten years or because of both of these reasons with some immeasurable statistical balance?

The information loop or cyclical feedback we are concerned with has to do with breaking down the standard medical textbook view that one thing necessarily follows from another, that a patient contracts this or that disease by doing this or that, or that this particular gene is responsible for this particular disease. As Yoxen (1983) reminded us, since we are dealing with systems of systems that transfer information among all the components of all the systems, there is no linear evolutionary trajectory we can follow. What appear as dead ends may end up opening new developmental venues and thereby fracture the continuity of one line of organic or biological development. This line of thought, we would like to emphasize, is relevant because it undermines any view of scientific or medical certainty the public may still be cherishing from their history of science textbooks. Perhaps there is here a broader belief-system problem of wishing for some general order in nature and in life, an order that could be fully comprehended and therefore fully predicted. Under such a circumstance, it would be reasonable to expect some level of certainty and some efficacy of medical intervention and treatment. Yes, we might need another century to collect the relevant data and reconfigure them within different and evolving frameworks, but this is merely a matter of time and not in principle an impossible option.

If medical certainty in the narrow and outdated sense of "knowing for sure" is nothing but a myth whose time has passed, as one appreciates the inherent fallibility of the field (see Gorovitz & MacIntyre 1976), then we might be willing to relinquish any expectation of practical certitude with regard to medical practice (even within a Kantian framework of the categorical imperative). Debates over moral certainty – over what is absolutely right or wrong, or over what is absolutely good or evil – cannot be fully resolved in this context. We mean neither to elaborate nor to resolve these debates here (but will devote Chapter 4 to these issues), but only to assert that we believe it difficult to accept any view of absolute certainty in the clinical setting, and therefore recommend jettisoning "rights language" considerations as inappropriate substitutes for deeper discussion of epistemological quandaries. We would agree, for example, that murdering a patient intentionally and without any reason is practically and socially evil and wrong; we would likewise agree that trying to save a patient's life based on the request of the patient is practically good and right. But these two cases do not require much elaboration outside the details of each particular case. One can fault the literature for being too complicated and obscure, but one must realize that most situations that have ethical components in medicine are not as simple as the two above-mentioned cases. The complication is usually caused not so much by the applicability of more than one moral principle or the inapplicability of all the moral principles as simply formulated but more, as we have tried to illustrate in Chapters 1 to 3, by ignorance of the epistemological, metaphysical and ontological frameworks that affect our thought and action.

As we mentioned above in relation to so-called alternative medical models or the therapies common in other continents of the world, there must be some level of tolerance and acceptance when it comes to medical treatment. What we have in mind here is not simply the pragmatic pressure to use whatever works no matter on what epistemological grounds it is based, but a deeper appreciation of the inevitable confluence of and conflict among different and incommensurable medical frameworks. In a recent case in Virginia, a judge found a legal compromise in the case of a teenager who sought to stop chemotherapy for his cancer. His parents would have been charged "with medical neglect for allowing him to seek alternative treatment from a clinic in Mexico" (Markon 2006: A1). Let us review some of the details of this case, because we believe that it can illustrate the kind of integrative bioethics we have in mind, where feedback affects treatment and can affect the choices parents and their children have when it comes to the unknowns of a cancer diagnosis. Perhaps because the courts intervened in this case, it also illustrates how legal and ethical concerns are always interdependent on what we know about a medical condition and the therapies that have been used in the past to treat it.

> [The teenager] was diagnosed with Hodgkin's disease last August after a mass was found on his neck. A pediatric oncologist at Children's Hospital of the King's Daughters in Norfolk recommended chemotherapy for the teenager and then, if needed, radiation. . . . An initial round of chemotherapy ravaged Abraham Cherrix, he and his parents have said, reducing his 6-foot frame to 122 pounds and causing his hair to fall out. After the therapy shrank his tumors but did not eliminate all signs of the disease, an oncologist at the Norfolk hospital recommended radiation and more chemotherapy. (*Ibid.*)

Obviously, the course of treatment seemed ineffective and the side-effects, as happens in many such cases, quite devastating. Because the parents sought an alternative, the case

> pitted parental rights against the government's obligation to protect the health of children. . . . Under state and federal court decisions, parents are usually allowed to make medical decisions for their children, legal and medical experts said. But some states, including Virginia, allow judges to override parental decisions if they believe a child's health is endangered. (*Ibid.*)

Should radiation be the only reasonable form of treatment, or can nutrition alone provide a cure to this teenager's cancer? Since no conclusive data are available as to the "best" treatment of cancer, what criteria should physicians recommend and patients use (or their proxy in case they are underage) and the courts of law enforce in treating cancer?

The fact that moral certainty is complex and tentative is not by itself an argument for ethical relativism. Members of the medical community may disagree on the limits, nature and justification of scientific principles as well as on their practical prioritization and significance, while still holding to a common ground on certain moral precepts. To argue against absolute medical certainty is not to state that a community cannot hold true certain beliefs about assessing the risks and benefits of this or that procedure or of this or that intervention and the price it is willing to pay to preserve life. That there exists conflict regarding how one should act in a moral world does not argue for a certain dogmatic view of the universe, nor does it doom one to accept random precepts concerning the appropriateness of public policy. This is precisely what we advocate in this book: an integrative approach that does not preclude the consideration of as many variables and factors as possible, and therefore leaves open the most appropriate solution in this context. As Kristin Shrader-Frechette (1980) acknowledges in the case of nuclear technology, one can find the links between military and civilian development and research funding, and even a certain congruence among practitioners in a certain field, so that a consensus can arise as to the risk of pushing for one sort of public policy rather than another. Risk assessment becomes an important and integral element in viewing scientific uncertainty in the case of medical practice. There may in fact be significant consensus as to what constitutes moral behaviour, allowing for judgements and actions agreeable to the moral community without at the same time necessitating an exposition in terms of moral certainty (Gorovitz 1985). Yet one should always be wary, as we have noted at the end of Chapter 1, of the possible drawbacks and dangers associated with medical practice. It is a question not only of experimentation on human subjects (from Nuremberg to IRBs), but even of basic research into the human genome – how can we prevent the risks associated with the accumulation of profound knowledge about humans and their genetic composition? (See in this context Annas & Elias 1992.) In short, if medical uncertainty is linked with risk assessment, it may be reasonable for the public to accept or reject certain procedures and protocols proposed by the medical community. Questions of scientific uncertainty quickly become moral considerations of public policy, whether they are theoretical (in the sense of basic research) or practical (in the sense of experimental therapies).

It seems reasonable to assume that most physicians will agree with our assertion concerning the difficulties with moral certainty. But not all would probably associate or link moral uncertainty with the inherent problems of medicine itself as a scientific enterprise. It seems that the myth of scientific certainty still carries the day among both practitioners and patients. The more sophisticated among them know that certainty in the sense of "knowing for sure" has been replaced with probabilistic terms. But even this change has made no difference to the view physicians hold of scientific certainty and the expectations of their patients. Although probable knowledge provides us with some notion of certainty, especially if the statistical data at hand are large enough, it is far from the notion of certainty concerning particular events or instances (Gorovitz 1982). To say that there is a 50 per cent chance that you will not survive a particular surgical procedure is not the same as being certain that you will die tomorrow (as would be the case if you were condemned to die by a court of law, for example, with no potential for appeal). Physicians, it seems to us, need not look to science exclusively for their views concerning certainty, but can draw their own conclusions from their medical practices that, as we showed above, include diagnosis, therapy and prognosis. And each of these may have different senses or levels of certainty associated with it. In doing so, they may be pioneers who help to reshape the nature of the scientific enterprise as a whole, rather than practitioners who yearn for the sanction of that enterprise. Theirs would be the informed case study whose empirical databases could transform the entire scientific discourse and culture. Although there may never be any scientific certainty even in its probabilistic terms concerning the diagnosis of disease and illnesses, as well as concerning their prognosis, this still should not paralyse clinical practices. For physicians are capable and are required to "do no harm and do the best they can" under these conditions of medical and moral uncertainty.

As we have outlined in the previous section, it seems that there is a weakening line of certainty when moving from diagnosis to treatment to prognosis. There are cases such as AIDS, where we know a lot about HIV but our treatments are less certain, particularly with regard to how they actually work genetically. Prognosis is tricky but probable; much depends on the individual's immune system in general and the infection trajectory in particular. Moral debates still rage about the public responsibility for bearing the costs of treatment, especially when those infected are portrayed as villains who deliberately contracted the disease (because of promiscuous gay lifestyles) rather than innocent victims of its unexpected onslaught (e.g. untested blood transfusion). But this way of seeing the situation is not necessarily the typical or the only one. Consider the case of glaucoma: we treat the pressure quite well (ask patients), but do not really understand the process that leads to the need for treatment (which drives patients crazy). Prognosis is very tricky, once again, except for stating that older patients are more likely to be inflicted with this condition. In this context, moral issues are quite secondary, if mentioned at all. It is here that we appreciate from yet another perspective the issues we raised in Chapter 2 in relation to knowing and doing in the medical field. Our practical knowledge and the success we have in treating patients may not be explicable in scientific terms or in the terms that render their success scientific (explanatory and predictive). Yet this should not be an impediment; instead, it should alert us to the kind of information loops we mentioned earlier. Certainty gained from treatment or the certainty of treatment might turn out to be a more significant epistemological starting point for theoretical discussion than this or that hypothesis about our bodies being "organic systems of systems".

Along similar lines of argument, we should break down the chronologically linear connection between diagnosis and treatment and appreciate the fact that when our treatment fails it might be either a poor diagnosis or a poor application of the treatment and not necessarily only one of them. Put differently, we should refrain from ascribing an *a priori* higher degree of certainty to diagnosis and assume that treatment is so personal that it is necessarily less prone to high degrees of certainty. If we were to take this suggestion seriously, we would listen to patients more attentively and collect their input as empirical data that ought to change the diagnosis and treatment of their and others' diseases. The point is to listen to patients not merely so as to prevent malpractice lawsuits and much more as a process that accumulates an informative and crucial set of data that impacts on how a patient can be better treated, namely as a process that ensures a feedback loop in the clinical settings. As we know, most diseases are multifactorial in the sense of coming about because of a constellation of variables and factors that contribute proportionately to the development and expression of a disease. The reductionist, single variable causal explanation might exist on many occasions but is not useful in all cases for all patients. Bleeding from a knife cut is easily identifiable even when the cause of the altercation or accident remains obscure. The treatment is straightforward in most cases (except for haemophiliacs or those with rare blood diseases), and the recovery time is fairly predictable. It therefore makes sense to consider as many variables and reports as possible so as to increase degrees of certainty in judging the onset of a disease and its eventual cure (when possible).

Perhaps the most useful advice we can garner from the preceding comments and discussions is a new appreciation of the central role that uncertainty plays in medicine. This is true not only because medicine is as much an art as a science, but also because science itself, and the biological sciences in particular, displays a level of uncertainty that is integral to its study and research, not to mention its practice. This is not to say that we know very little about our bodies and our health, but instead to say that what we know is prone to be revised and reconsidered, re-evaluated based on additional information or what we call feedback loops. As we explore the limits of our medical knowledge, we discover new ways of thinking about how we can heal people or treat their pain. And as they become our sources of information, as their treatment is examined and refined over time, we appreciate whatever errors we have made in the past and improve upon them for the future.

4

A new ethics of medical practice

As we survey some of the epistemological issues raised in medicine, we come to realize that they arise out of specific cultural concerns (social, economic and political) and have the power to transform them. An excellent example is the outcome of the Nuremberg Trials after the Second World War with regard to medical experimentation without informed consent. Institutional review boards became mandatory in the USA and Europe because of this re-examination and as such demonstrate how the ethical dimensions of contemporary western culture must be viewed against the backdrop of debates about scientific knowledge acquisition and application. Put another way, bioethics depends much on philosophical reflection and the kind of self-conscious feedback loops that inform future behaviour. Given this, it is time to rethink our approaches in bioethics, thereby fostering a new ethics of medical practice. One of the conclusions we draw is that as medicine is a context-bound discipline, so is bioethics. This insight leads us to argue that any account of bioethics that sets itself forth as the definitive methodology to use in the health care setting is questionable. Bioethical discourses are themselves evolving bodies of knowledge and values, which are set within particular historical, cultural contexts. They are integrative – within time, settings and lives – thus leading us to offer our suggestions for medical practice using an "integrative bioethics".

The plurality of medical knowledge

In order to contextualize our own proposals with regard to what should be done in the bioethical domain, a domain we acknowledged is understudied from the perspective of its epistemological foundation, we would like to rehearse some ideas and issues related to the complexity of biology in general and medicine in particular. One leading exponent of the philosophy of biology is Ernst Mayr (1982, 1997). In his numerous texts, he reminds us that when we deal with living organisms we should refrain from using the metaphors and models we are accustomed to use in physics, for example. In his words,

> Living organisms form a hierarchy of ever more complex systems. From molecules, cells, and tissues, through whole organisms, populations, and species. In each higher system, characteristics emerge that could not have been predicted from a knowledge of the components.
>
> (Mayr 1997: xvi)

Now this notion of emergence, as it is commonly called nowadays, may not be restricted to the living sciences, and could be extended to other areas of study. Yet, if fully understood in relation to biology and the growth of organisms, it would defy any attempt at reductionism (the view that every phenomenon can be taken apart to its smallest components so as to study how they work together). Mayr and his cohorts are concerned with the ability to study biology like all the other sciences, or, as some of them appreciate it, figuring out whether or not biology is an autonomous field of research different enough from all other sciences that it warrants its own methods of inquiry (*ibid.*: 30ff.). Does biology exhibit the same kinds of universal claims that mechanics does? Does biology discover the kinds of laws of nature that are immutable and that bind all phenomena no matter what their specific environments? Can biological facts be quantified in the same manner as physical ones? It is with these questions in mind that Mayr concludes that "In biology a plurality of causal factors, combined with probabilism in the chain of events, often makes it very difficult, if not impossible, to determine *the* cause of a given phenomenon" (*ibid.*: 68). So, when multiple causes are attributed, namely no singular cause can be affirmed with certainty, controversies may arise. When they do, says Mayr, they may be temporarily settled not by finding binding facts that overshadow the others, but by forging a new theory or hypothesis or explanation that uses elements from all the competing explanations (*ibid.*: 69).

Mayr stays close to the view of biology as a science and explains what makes it unique among all other sciences and what makes it worthy of continued interest, especially along Darwinian lines. In doing so, he also explains the kind of diversity of ideas and explanatory models that remain acceptable in the field, namely the basic realization that many causes contribute to a certain effect, and that a certain effect can have multiple causes. This is baffling to those who wish to find a linear and simplified view of one cause leading to one effect. But as biology celebrates the emergence of properties and effects that could not have been predicted from any set of variables or causes, it is therefore bound to display a richness of diversity and pluralism not seen in many other fields of research that focus on natural phenomena. In his words:

> In short, there are multiple possible solutions for many evolutionary challenges, even though all of them are compatible with the Darwinian paradigm. The lesson one must learn from this pluralism is that in evolutionary biology sweeping generalizations are rarely correct. Even when something occurs "usually," this does not mean that it must occur always. (*Ibid.*: 206)

The diversity and the plurality of biology as related to medicine are fundamental traits that ought to be epistemologically realized in order to have a more reasonable and useful posture when it gets to the clinical setting. The faith we have in science at times translates improperly to biology and medicine as if they, as scientific enterprises, can provide us with clear-cut answers to complex questions about our health. We should note that, for Mayr, science is complex for epistemological, not social, reasons. But having shifted our attention from a reductionist, deterministic model of science to a complex, emerging one, Mayr also shifts our attention to the peculiarities of biology and by extension medicine.

Richard Lewontin is in full agreement with Mayr's shift, but for him this is true because we forget to notice that science itself is a social institution, prone to be driven by certain ideological commitments that remain undetected by practitioners and laypeople alike (Lewontin 1993: 3ff.). As he considers the treatment of cancer, Lewontin reminds us that "Medicine remains, despite all the talk of scientific medicine, essentially an empirical process in which one does what works" (*ibid.*: 5). This conclusion flies in the face of the standard "ideology of modern science" that "makes the atom or individual the causal source of all the properties of larger collections" (*ibid.*: 12–13). This is true also when one speaks of genes as isolated entities whose causal effects can be traced, because one is still captured by the "*ideology of biological determinism*" (*ibid.*: 23), the view that genes determine specific traits and diseases that can be found in individual organisms. It is here where Lewontin insists on distinguishing between agents and causes. His example is the following:

> Asbestos fibers and pesticides are the agents of disease and disability, but it is illusory to suppose that if we eliminate these particular irritants that the disease will go away, for other similar irritants will take their place. . . . Asbestos and cotton lint fibers are not the causes of cancer. They are agents of social causes, of social formations that determine the nature of our productive and consumptive lives, and in

the end it is only through changes in those social forces that we can get to the root problems of health. The transfer of causal power from social relations into inanimate agents that then seem to have a power and life of their own is one of the major mystifications of science and its ideologies. (*Ibid.*: 45–6)

Because Lewontin appreciates the difference between causes and agents and between accepting both on the different social and scientific levels of discussion in which they appear, he can alert us to appreciate the misconceptions we import into health provision and the therapies that are deemed useful. This alert remains relevant in the gene age, where, as Lewontin suggests, we err when "talking about the human gene sequence as if all human beings were alike. In fact, there is an immense amount of variation from normal individual to normal individual in the amino acid sequence of their proteins because a given protein may have a variety of amino acid compositions without impairing its function" (*ibid.*: 49).

Just as Mayr insisted on explaining living organisms in terms of their diversity and the plurality of explanatory models we can provide for their behaviour (and malfunction), so does Lewontin insist on explaining living organisms in terms of their internal and external development. For Lewontin this means that:

A living organism at any moment in its life is the unique consequence of a developmental history that results from the interaction of and determination by internal and external forces. The external forces, what we usually think of as "environment," are themselves partly a consequence of the activities of the organism itself as it produces and consumes the conditions of its own existence. Organisms do not find the world in which they develop. They make it. Reciprocally, the internal forces are not autonomous, but act in response to the external. Part of the internal chemical machinery of a cell is only manufactured when external conditions demand it. For example, the enzyme that breaks down the sugar, lactose, to provide energy for bacterial growth is only manufactured by bacterial cells when they detect the presence of lactose in their environment.   (*Ibid.*: 63–4)

Since there is an ongoing reciprocity between internal and external forces, between the behaviour of genes and the environment in which they develop, it is difficult, if not impossible, to arrest its development or its effects in order to find a precise causal relation between its mutation, for example, and a specific set of symptoms we associate with a disease. In Lewontin's words:

> The gene whose mutant form leads to cystic fibrosis has been located, isolated, and sequenced. The protein encoded by the gene has been deduced. Unfortunately, it looks like a lot of other proteins that are part of cell structure, so it is hard to know what to do next. The mutation leading to Tay-Sachs disease is even better understood because the enzyme specified by the gene has a quite specific and simple function, but no one has suggested a therapy. On the other hand, the gene mutation causing Huntington's disease has eluded exact location, and no biochemical or specific metabolic defect has been found for a disease that results in catastrophic degeneration of the central nervous system in every carrier of the defective gene.   (*Ibid.*: 66)

The message here supports our critique of the standard classification of diagnosis, therapy and prognosis not only in terms of efficacy, but also in terms of how little we know when we think that the scientific framework into which medical ailments are lodged seems to provide a modicum of certainty. Put differently, the faith we have in the knowledge we can gain from genetic research seems unwarranted. At times our therapies work without us knowing exactly why; at times our knowledge of the causes and agents that contribute to a disease are sophisticated and accurate, but we remain powerless to do anything about it. Reductionism, as already noted, is itself an ideology in so far as it invokes a belief that once we know the components of our bodies and their interactions we will be able to know everything about how our bodies work. As Lewontin concludes, "When we free ourselves of the ideological biases of atomism and reductionism and look squarely at the actual relations between organisms and the world around them, we find a much richer set of relations" (*ibid.*: 109). It is in this sense, then, that Lewontin recommends viewing the organism's interaction with its environment constructively, as if "the environment of organisms is coded in their DNA" (*ibid.*: 112).

When a group of British researchers attempted an ethnographic study of clinical settings that relied on genetic information for diagnosis and treatment, they found what Mayr and Lewontin suggest: life is more complicated than we thought, and any philosophical or ideological or epistemological foundations are bound to fall short of what actually happens with people who are sick. In their words, "the relationship between laboratory science and clinical inference is a practical matter for the participants themselves" (Latimer *et al.* 2006: 607). These researchers focused on dysmorphology classifications as they are based on or can be traced to "two main genetic causes . . . as single-gene defects and chromosomal abnormalities" (*ibid.*: 608). Since the classifications themselves are prone to ambiguity, they found that there is an inherent ambiguity and uncertainty with regard to the test results obtained in cases where physicians rely on laboratories in order to help them to diagnose what ails a patient (*ibid.*: 617), so that "in the field of dysmorphology, it is difficult to give a definitive genetic diagnosis" (*ibid.*: 619). Hence, they say, "molecular tests themselves call for more clinical interpretation rather than less" (*ibid.*: 621).

Perhaps at this point we should recall some of our earlier comments on the age of postmodernism, where a plurality of ideas and theories are bound to remain as a way of living and interacting with ourselves and our environments. The faith in a unitary, universal, objective and permanent universe is untenable when what we find out about our own bodies is the diverse ways in which their components and basic elements remain open to changes and developments in relation to their immediate and remote environ-ments. If uncertainty is the hallmark of our scientific and medical knowledge, then we ought to pay more attention to how we react to this, how we must change our belief systems and our behaviour to acknowledge this condition. It is from this that we draw our assessments of the ethical dimensions of human behaviour and prospects, and to which we must now turn.

If we agree that there is neither absolute scientific certainty (and by extension) nor absolute moral certainty in all matters concern-ing medicine, we suggest not giving up and receding to some naive sense of scientific and moral relativism. Instead, we suggest forging ahead with a middle ground, so to speak, that is both informed and proactive, engaged with the practical situations as they arise and concerned not to promise too much or too little in the way of alleviation of pain and suffering. In pursuing this middle ground, we revisit the notion of responsibility as a more useful category (rather than rights language) with which to provide some sugges-tions and guidelines for the field of medicine. First, we can safely say that health care providers need not feel responsible for the lack of certainty in medicine. This uncertainty is both methodologi-cally unavoidable and practically a fact of life. Although it may be disheartening to both physicians and patients, this uncertainty should not be viewed as the result of the physicians' own doing; they have to work under conditions of uncertainty just as meteoro-logists must predict the weather under conditions of uncertainty. This, of course, does not mean that anything goes (in Feyerabend's sense), because they still must attempt to retrieve any evidence that has any bearing on reducing the conditions of uncertainty, or on turning these conditions closer to more certain ones (in a prob-abilistic sense; see Colton 1974).

Secondly, we can say that there still remains professional respons-ibility associated with the administration of medical care. This professional responsibility consists primarily of the standard codes of ethics as formulated by Hippocrates as well as by several medical societies and health associations since that time. These codes of

professional ethics make physicians responsible for certain pro-
cedural matters as well as certain ethical modes of behaviour.
Regardless of any scientific uncertainty associated with medicine,
physicians must be responsible for doing the best they can under
the circumstances. They can devote their attention to providing the
best data available and use the best techniques so far developed,
explaining to patients and administrators the limits of their knowledge and the extent to which so-called redundant tests and procedures may be crucial.

Thirdly, the concept of personal responsibility is interwoven
with the concept of accountability. It is arguable that because
medicine provides physicians only with probable knowledge and
that they must rely on their own experiences as well as on those of
their colleagues, physicians should turn professional accountability and responsibility into a personal matter. That is, physicians
should realize that their personal relationship with their patients
determines the scope of their responsibility (from taking medical
histories to identifying with the patient's plight and concerns). This
strong personal commitment should be *prima facie* morally binding regardless of any financial arrangements that might have some
bearing on this relationship from other perspectives. For, once the
relationship is established between patient and physician or nurse,
it provides the moral foundations upon which accountability and
responsibility are defined (Konold 1978). In this sense, then, the
realization that medicine cannot provide us with scientific certainty makes it clear that the individual patient relies on the individual medical administration and the goodwill of physicians. This
sort of individual reliance necessitates a more stressful sort of
responsibility heaved upon the physician's shoulders, but one that
would in the long run alleviate some of the pressure that comes
from unrealistic expectations and ongoing frustration with the
shortcomings of the provision of health care.

Summarizing the three major kinds of responsibilities of medical practice associated with scientific uncertainty allows us to view
the concept of responsibility for individual physicians in new ways.
Individual physicians, one could argue, can opt to choose one of

two alternatives. On the one hand, they can use the idea of scientific uncertainty to shirk all responsibility and claim that all they can be accountable for is to "do the best they can". That is, they cannot be held responsible for the death of their patients, because there are always bound to be so many unknown factors obscuring their ability to diagnose accurately as well as to treat their patients in ways that will guarantee recovery. On the other hand, physicians can acknowledge the difficulties associated with uncertainty in medicine, while accepting full responsibility for their activities to the extent that the variables are within their control. This is not to say that they must feel responsible for any patient who has contracted some rare disease, which is incurable, and who eventually dies. We think that it is no longer possible for physicians, regardless of the psychological pressures associated with medicine, to opt for either alternative. They must take full responsibility for providing their best services for any given patient, making their utmost efforts to help patients and treat them, and employ the best available scientific data relevant for the medical care of their patients – disregarding, and at the same time being fully aware of, the inherent uncertainty both in medicine as science and in morality.

There is a sense in which we think that most physicians have adopted alternative views concerning their responsibility towards the medical care of their patients. This adoption of competing views concerning responsibility eventually causes physicians to feel a psychological tension, which is difficult to trace or reconcile. On the one hand, physicians are compulsive in their attempts to amass as many medical data as possible so as to provide the best possible medical care – namely, they wish to know everything they can to assure that their clinical behaviour is appropriate. On the other hand, they realize quite quickly that they cannot internalize all the medical knowledge stored within libraries and computers – and that their medical knowledge is incomplete, imperfect and uncertain.

Since this is not a psychological analysis, we refrain from elaborating on the anguish, ambivalence and frustration physicians may be feeling on one level or another. But, as shown elsewhere in the context of scientists and engineers (Sassower 1997), we think it important to trace some of the causes that have led to this situa-tion. As we noted earlier, some of these causes are epistemic in nature and have to do with scientific inquiry of any sort, including, of course, medicine. If medical practice is to be handled rationally – given its problematic epistemic foundation – we may have to help to change the public view of its scientific status. This change in perspective may allow us to re-examine our views concerning the responsibility of physicians. We may wish them to feel less responsible for their inability to provide us with certain medical knowledge, yet we may want them to accept full responsibility for their clinical behaviour. Scientific uncertainty in medicine does not imply medical irresponsibility in the hospital.

Although Alfred I. Tauber's main focus is on the notion of autonomy and its philosophical foundation and medical application, there is still an important reminder that physicians work within a framework of professionalism wherein they "are trained experts essentially committed to addressing the biomedical problems at hand" (Tauber 2005: 2–3). He also reminds us that physicians have "multiple responsibilities" (*ibid*.: 5) and therefore speaks of "*moral epistemology* – moral, because clinical evaluation and care are value-laden, and epistemological, because medicine expresses and employs a form of knowledge" (*ibid*.: 9). He continues:

> Clinical science scrutinizes and treats disease and the doctor treats the person; this difference is what makes medicine more than a natural science, for its practitioners must synthesize the various strands of its faculties in the service of the patient. In short, I maintain that the glue holding together the various epistemological strands of contemporary medicine is of a personal moral character, and what we seek is a better understanding of medicine's moral epistemology as it is guided by responsibility, namely, an ethics of care." (*Ibid*.: 10)

Because Tauber believes that "Autonomy is inadequate, by itself, to account for medicine's moral calling because of two failings" (*ibid*.:

18), he also appreciates that the atomistic view of people (much like Lewontin above) is insufficient for moral behaviour. Instead, he recommends, "The strategy employed here is to move the rights-dominated arguments into a different framework, where moral relations between atomistic individuals are configured not as the rights of those in conflict but rather as the responsibilities of persons in mutually supporting relationships" (*ibid.*: 25). It is here that he also explains how "positivism and reductionism" have governed the medical profession, instead of another set of values (*ibid.*: Ch. 1).

Tauber echoes our sentiment when he concedes that "Clinical care demands full attention to both domains – scientific and moral" (*ibid.*: 49). Because of his appreciation of the linkage of these domains, he can more readily incorporate the one into the other, with the notion of uncertainty, as we have developed it in Chapter 3, remaining paramount. As he says:

> Yet good clinicians function easily in this climate of uncertainty, because they have internalized methods for dealing with partial data and extrapolations from dissimilar clinical scenarios. They are increasingly aware that the best treatment strategies are largely intuited from experience and involve hidden judgments that are biased in ways usually unrecognized, and as noted, are extrapolated with the aid of measures hardly supported by rigorous analysis. Nevertheless, decisions must be made. (*Ibid.*: 52)

But having to make decisions within this multilayered framework does not mean that any function by itself remains isolated; they are all interrelated. There are three models of the physician–patient relationship: bureaucrat, scientist and magician (*ibid.*: 62). In the light of this, he concludes:

> So it is generally acknowledged that doctors err on the side of failing to admit doubt in their field of expertise. This is, of course highly ironic inasmuch as uncertainty

in medicine is omnipresent. But that is not the psychological relevant fact: doubt is perceived to signify a lack of
knowledge.

(*Ibid.*: 64, citing here Pellegrino and Thomasma 1981)

This is his logic of his argument about ethics: "To be moral, we
must be responsible for our actions. To be responsible, we must be
able to choose freely. To choose freely, we must be autonomous.
And the tool for human autonomy was human rationality" (*ibid.*:
97). He uses Onora O'Neill (2002) to transform the Kantian notion
of "individual autonomy" to more socially and culturally based
notions of "principles autonomy" that evolve over time and that
are communal even when addressing the individual actor (Tauber
2005: 105, 121). This means, for example, that when a patient signs
an informed consent form, this act in itself is an act of assuming
responsibility for delegating responsibility to someone else, someone the patient can trust (*ibid.*: 133–43). This may sound a bit con-
fusing, but the conscious and deliberate consideration to delegate
one's decision-making to a professional is significant and should
be seriously considered as a way of interacting in the medical community without contention or conflict.

One of the reasons we have used Tauber's text is because it is a
recent attempt to deal with some of the issues we are interested in,
namely how responsible adults ought to interact in the medical
framework, appreciating the context of their decision-making processes. Moreover, when we first encountered this text we thought
it could also deal more subtly with the concerns we have with a
rights-based ethical approach to health care provision. Admittedly,
Tauber makes some of the moves we endorse in terms of looking
for a broader context with which to make bioethical judgements.
Yet he still fails to encompass the epistemological quandaries we
have outlined throughout our book. Perhaps we ought to review
some of the standard bioethical discourses and their critiques so
as to sharpen the edges that delineate our presentations from all
others.

Leading bioethical discourses

With Tauber's recommendations in mind and our view regarding the plurality of medical epistemologies, we turn now to a closer look at the field of bioethics and the challenges it faces. Typically when one thinks of values in medicine, one thinks of the host of ethical appeals that arise. Abortion, lifestyle choices, physician-assisted suicide and health care delivery command our attention in part because of the power of medicine to transform patients' lives in ways previously not possible or imagined. The discipline of bioethics developed in the late twentieth century along with major advancements in medical science and technology, such as found in intensive care units, and in response to early twentieth-century medical events that defied the boundaries of moral behaviour, such as found in Nazi Germany. As with the earlier field of medical ethics, fostered by the likes of eighteenth-century clinicians Benjamin Rush and Thomas Percival, its primary focus has been on the doctor–patient relationship and norms for behaviour. But bioethics differs from the traditional medical ethics by looking at questions that arise outside of the strictly clinical context (e.g. research ethics) and engaging in interdisciplinary dialogue involving philosophers, scientists and public policy experts. In this respect, bioethics has in some sense pioneered interdisciplinary work in the late twentieth and early twenty-first centuries (Illingworth & Parmet 2006: 2). It is this emphasis on interdisciplinary studies – on concerns outside science and medicine proper, including social, economic and political ones – that provides a rich base for a new ethics in medical practice, as we shall soon see.

There is no doubt that Nazi Germany was instrumental in leading us to rethink our ethical approaches in medicine. Prior to Nazi Germany, few questions were asked about how physicians and scientists treated their patients/subjects. Despite some exceptions, such as one voiced by Bartolomaeus Fumus in 1538, stating that physicians commit sin when they "make experiments and such like, by which the patient is exposed to grave danger" (Amundsen 1981: 35), there are numerous counter-examples. Pasteur tested his new rabies vaccine on a young child exposed to rabies without securing informed consent. Jenner tested versions of live anthrax immunization on milkmaids without full disclosure of intent. Things change with Nazi Germany, when experiments perpetuated by the Nazi doctors on concentration camp victims came to light, despite there being a research ethics code in place (Sass 1983). These and others formed the basis for the Doctors' Trials, one of the postwar hearings held by the Allies at Nuremberg in the late 1940s. Following the trial, judges issued the Nuremberg Code, which proclaimed that "voluntary consent of the human subject is absolutely essential" (Permissible Medical Experiments n.d.: 181) for the use of a human being in research. The Code also required that all experiments should be "conducted as to avoid all unnecessary physical and mental suffering and injury" and should never be undertaken if there "is an a priori reason to believe that death or disabling injury will occur" (*ibid.*: 182).

Where Nuremberg rejects any balancing of the individual's right to consent with the greater good of society, the World Medical Association's Helsinki Declaration (1964) departs by permitting surrogate consent when individuals are themselves incapable of giving informed consent. As it says, "Where physical or mental incapacity makes it impossible to obtain informed consent, or when the subject is a minor, permission from the responsible relative replaces that of the subject in accordance with national legislation" (*ibid.*: I, 11). It also distinguishes between non-therapeutic and clinical research (*ibid.*: II and III) and permits non-therapeutic research in cases involving "purely scientific" (*ibid.*: III) applications. Nevertheless, under Helsinki, researchers are never allowed to place the interest of science and society over the well-being of the subject (*ibid.*: III, 4).

Despite the rules promulgated by the Nuremberg Code and Helsinki Declaration, scientists throughout the world continued to use individuals in research without their full, voluntary consent. One of the more blatant uses was the so-called Tuskegee Study conducted by the United States Public Health Service (Jones 1981). In this study, the United States Pubic Health Service decided to study 400 "untreated male Negro subjects" infected with syphilis living in rural Macon County, Georgia, to observe the course of their disease. Individuals who were enrolled were neither informed about the nature of their disease or the study, nor given state-of-the-art treatment, even when modern antibiotics became available.

Public responses to these and others studies in the United States led to the Code of Federal Regulations for the Protection of Human Subjects (45 CFR Pt 46) (2005) that governs the use of human subjects in US federally funded research protocols as well as in clinical trials in the Food and Drug Administration's (FDA's) licensing process. These rules call for mandatory institutional review boards, or IRBs, which are charged with determining whether a proposed research protocol provides for informed consent, utilizes an equitable selection of subjects, protects subject privacy and is designed in such a way that the risks are minimized and are proportional to the anticipated benefits (*ibid.*: 46.111). Note that the guidelines do not require a strict adherence to patient rights; they allow for a weighing of patient rights with patient welfare, similar to Helsinki. As the regulations say, "Informed consent will be sought from each prospective subject or the subject's legally authorized representative" (*ibid.*: 46.111, 4). Yet, in contrast to Helsinki and Nuremberg, 45 CFR Pt 46 places greater emphasis on equitable distribution of the benefits and burdens of research. As it states, "Selection of subjects is equitable. In making this assessment the IRB should take into account the purposes of the research and the setting in which the research will be conducted and should be particularly cognizant of the special problems of research involving vulnerable populations" (*ibid.*: s. 46.111, [a] [3]).

This brief overview of Nuremberg, Helsinki and 45 CFR Pt 46 provides a window into the language and assumptions of twentieth-century bioethics. Commitments to patient rights, patient welfare and just distribution frame these and subsequent debates in bioethical discussions. In the late twentieth century, and drawing on the contributions of those in the history of moral philosophy, numerous bioethicists began to draw up what has come to be known as the mantra of bioethical principles. An initial formulation occurs in what is called *The Belmont Report* (National Commission 1978) and includes the principles of respect for person (recognition of human rights), beneficence (acting to promote another's good) and justice (the fair allocation of resources). Although initially developed to govern ethical research involving human subjects, these principles soon became the buzz-terms and guideposts for behaviour and actions in western medicine. Tom Beauchamp and James Childress's best-selling *Principles of Biomedical Ethics* (2001) incorporates and expands these principles using the language of autonomy, nonmaleficence, beneficence and justice.

Consider these widely recognized bioethical principles as formulated by Beauchamp and Childress as well as others and their applications in closer detail. The principle of respect for autonomy instructs each person to acknowledge another's "right to hold views, to make choices, and to take actions based on personal values and beliefs" (*ibid.*: 63). It requires not interfering with another's attitudes and actions as well as some obligation to build up or maintain another's "capacities for autonomous choice while helping to allay fears and other conditions that destroy or disrupt their autonomous actions" (*ibid.*: 63). Concretely put, in medicine, autonomy grounds truth-telling, respect for the privacy of others, protection of confidential information and the practice of informed consent (*ibid.*: 65).

Great emphasis is placed on informed consent in contemporary medicine. The term "informed consent" appears in the 1950s, but it is not until the 1970s that the idea receives detailed attention. Beauchamp and Childress argue that a full understanding of the moral character of informed consent entails considering the following seven elements:

I Threshold elements (preconditions)
   1 Competence (to understand and decide)
   2 Voluntariness (in deciding)

II Information elements
   3 Disclosure (of material information)
   4 Recommendation (of a plan)
   5 Understanding (of 3 and 4)
III Consent elements
   6 Decision (in favour of a plan)
   7 Authorization (of the chosen plan)   (*Ibid*.: 80)

In other words, treating persons as autonomous agents entails their having the ability (1) to understand information, (2) to choose, (3) to process material information, (4) to design a plan, (5) to understand the information and plan, (6) to decide in favour of one plan over another and (7) to authorize their chosen plan.

All these elements receive lengthy attention in the bioethics literature. For purposes of remaining focused on autonomy, let us take a closer look at the importance and challenges of disclosure in the clinical setting. How much medical information should be disclosed in order to provide for an appropriate basis for decision-making? Consider the possibilities: providing information according to: a professional practice standard (what a clinician would want or need); a reasonable person standard (what the "average" person would want or need); or a subjective standard (what the individual him- or herself would want or need). Although the US courts have typically supported the reasonable person standard (Cutter & Shelp 1991), discussion continues about what the appropriate standard(s) should be, especially in the light of increased access to medical information on the Internet and through the media. And is it ever morally permissible for a clinician to withhold information, an act called "therapeutic privilege", in cases where the information may bring more harm than benefit to the patient? At what point should a dying patient be told his or her prognosis? Should patients seeking genetic testing be informed that the results also affect family members who are not yet patients? These and related challenges remain centrepoints in bioethical discussions in this day and age of recognizing patient autonomy and rights and continuing the legacy of Locke and Kant and their interest in grounding moral philosophy of a notion of respect for person (e.g. Katz 1984a).

Before we continue, it should be noted that while our previous discussion of Tauber's concern with autonomy and responsibility can be framed in communitarian terms, the history of the use of these terms in the bioethics literature is framed differently. For example, Beauchamp and Childress's understanding of autonomy is construed individualistically. An individual is a self-determining entity with rights and duties that are a function of his or her individual relations to another individual in the community. This is different, of course, from an approach that finds the community as a whole a determining factor in decision-making or that binds all individual interactions in the light of their effects on the community.

A second principle in bioethics that receives significant attention is nonmaleficence. The principle of nonmaleficence "asserts an obligation not to inflict harm on others" (Beauchamp & Childress 2001: 113). It involves intentionally *refraining* from actions that cause harm. The principle of nonmaleficence supports specific moral actions in medicine such as refraining from killing, causing pain or suffering, incapacitating another, causing offence and depriving another of the goods of life (*ibid.*: 117). The principle has come to be closely associated with the maxim *primum non nocere*, "above all [or first] do not harm", a notion rooted in Hippocratic thinking.

Several guidelines are found in medicine that appeal to the principle of nonmaleficence. These include those involving withholding and withdrawing life-sustaining treatment, setting boundaries on the use of artificial feeding and life-sustaining medical technologies, and distinguishing between ordinary and extraordinary care. The early twenty-first century will be known for its debates on death and dying; not only do humans live longer, medicine is able to intervene in ways that astound even the veteran in health care. Patients spend a significant amount of funds during the last few months of life and the medical–industrial complex grows at a rate previously unseen. Yet not all individuals agree with using resources in these ways. Questions such as "when is enough treatment enough?" and "whose life is it anyway?" spawn interest in the development of advance directives (beginning in 1975 in the United States) that allow adult patients to specify the limits of care at the end of life. "Classic" right-to-die cases, such as Quinlan and Kevorkian become subjects for analysis and discussion (Pence 2000). The Netherlands, Belgium and Oregon legalize physician-assisted suicide and others in the United States debate this possibility.

Whereas the principle of nonmaleficence calls for refrain from action, the principle of beneficence, the third principle, calls for an active sense of promoting the well-being of another much in the tradition of Mill's emphasis on utility in moral philosophy. The principle supports *general* rules of moral actions such as protecting and defending the rights of others, preventing harm from occurring to others, removing conditions that will cause harm to others, helping persons with disabilities and rescuing persons in danger (Beauchamp & Childress 2001: 167). It also supports *specific* rules directed at persons such as children, friends and patients. Beauchamp and Childress argue that a person X has a specific obligation of beneficence towards person Y if and only if each of the following conditions is satisfied:

- Y is at risk of significance loss or damage to life or health or some other major interest.
- X's action is needed (singly or in concert with others) to prevent this loss or damage.
- X's action (singly or in concert with each other) has a high probability of preventing it.
- X's action would not present significant risks, costs or burdens to X.
- The benefit that Y can be expected to gain outweighs any harms, costs or burdens that X is likely to incur (*ibid*.: 171).

Clearly, in thinking through the requirements of beneficent actions, much turns on what constitute "significant risks, costs or burdens", for which informal and formal techniques have been developed. Informal techniques "include expert judgments, based on the most reliable data that can be assembled and analogical reasoning based on precedents" (*ibid.*: 194). These techniques are typically used in IRB protocol, where the investigator must state the risks to subjects and probable benefits to both subjects and society and justify how the probable benefits outweigh the risks to the subject. Formal techniques involve the manipulation of "numbers in order to express the objective probability that a research protocol will produce a net benefit" (*ibid.*: 194). This is a sophisticated body of techniques, much too much to review here, but for purposes of illustration involving cost-effectiveness analysis (CEA, which measures the benefits in non-monetary terms such as years of life, quality-adjusted-life-years or QUALYS and cases of disease), cost–benefit analysis (CBA, which measures both the benefits and costs in monetary terms) and risk–benefit analysis (RBA, which evaluates risks in relation to probable benefits).

For purposes of illustration, consider risk–benefit analysis in the regulation of drugs. In the 1990s, and in response to the rise of AIDS and calls from interest groups, the US FDA developed mechanisms to provide expanded access to experimental drugs, such as zidovudine (AZT). In its medical risk–benefit analysis for expedited approval, the FDA sought to determine, first, whether the drug's benefits outweighed its risks and, secondly, whether there was a need for more evidence about those benefits and risks, in view of the disease's seriously debilitating or life-threatening conditions. Having concluded that the benefits outweighed the risks, and recognizing the limits of what was known, the FDA authorized its use, much to the applause of AIDS activists. In another case, not involving expedited approval, and much to the shock of thirteen million American women, the FDA stopped research on hormone replacement therapy (HRT) after it showed that the popular drug of choice for menopausal women, Prempro, leads to a 0.3 to 0.4 per cent increase in heart attacks, strokes, blood clots and breast cancer in women (Cowley & Springen 2002). Here again, careful risk–benefit calculations are employed to establish whether a drug is considered safe on the market.

The fourth principle, that of justice, guides our thinking about what is fair, equitable and appropriate treatment in the light of what is due or owed to persons. Justice is one of the oldest moral principles, dating back to the great works of Plato and Aristotle. Today, justice is commonly distinguished as distributive, criminal and rectificatory. Distributive justice "refers to fair, equitable, and appropriate distribution determined by justified norms that structure the terms of social cooperation. Its scope includes policies that allot diverse benefits and burdens, such as property, resources, taxation, privileges, and opportunities" (Beauchamp & Childress 2001: 226). Criminal justice addresses the appropriate infliction of punishment as set forth by a body of law. Rectificatory justice attends to fair compensation for transaction problems such as breach of contracts and malpractice. In medicine, and especially in health care delivery, justice commands much attention.

Consider some options for material principles of justice, specifically distributive justice, and their outcomes as health care delivery models (e.g. Fletcher 1960). Without being exhaustive, resources can be distributed to persons according to: a communal standard; equal allocation; what will maximize societal benefits and minimize harms; and free-market exchange. Such distributions lead to very different kinds of health care delivery systems, including: a nationalized health care system in which health care providers and administrators are directly employed (as found in Britain) or in which a combination of government-supported and private providers operates (as found in Canada); government-funded vouchers for everyone; a mandatory employer-provided insurance or plan, with government-sponsorship of plans for other segments of society (as proposed in Massachusetts and San Francisco) or a heavily assisted free market, which includes government-funded insurance for direct provision of selected segments of the population and incentives for work-related health insurance plans (as found presently in the USA); and a fee-for-service system (an option found in all developed countries). Debates over which health care delivery model meets the demands of justice are anything but settled (Menzel 1992).

The principle of justice is also operative in current challenges about our response to emerging infections and bioterrorism. When bioethics emerged as a field in the 1970s, many health care professionals thought that the days of mass epidemics were over. Immunizations had been shown to be successful in the control of polio, measles, mumps and rubella, to name a few. Bioethicists turned their attention to research practices and reproductive rights in the 1970s, death with dignity in the 1980s and health care delivery in the 1990s. But HIV infection led many to reconsider their attention – or lack thereof. AIDS, along with Lyme disease, hantavirus, West Nile fever, SARS and bird flu, emerged and were recognized in our world for the first time. In addition, and in part because of antibiotic resistance, familiar infections such as tuberculosis and other viral infections became more prevalent. How ought we to respond? Who ought to pay? Are we no longer able simply to think about health care delivery in terms of national borders? The list of queries involving justice goes on.

In the early twenty-first century, the threats posed by emerging diseases are enhanced by the possibility of bioterrorism. The contamination of US mail in October 2001 with anthrax and the evidence of Saddam Hussein's use of toxic agents against members of minority groups leads to a re-evaluation of national and international responses to bioterrorism. With plenty of reflection on AIDS in tow, and stories of early twentieth-century responses to tuberculosis retold, attention turns as well to what constitutes appropriate quarantine practices and disclosure policies in cases of infectious diseases. Again, how ought we to respond? Who pays? What restrictions can and ought to be mandated? Who ought to monitor such activities? How ought conflicts between and among borders be resolved? Again, the list goes on.

There is no doubt that the principle approach has set the framework for late twentieth-century and early twenty-first-century thinking in bioethics. As our discussion indicates, it has provided a useful tool to classify and address many of the large problems that confront us in contemporary western society. The principles of autonomy, nonmaleficence, beneficence and justice clearly lend them-

selves to addressing a sundry of patient rights, welfare and alloca-
tional quandaries. With its roots in the history of moral philosophy,
the principle approach draws from the great works of Plato, Aristotle,
Kant, Mill and others for its philosophical depth and cogency. It is
no wonder that it has set the stage in contemporary bioethics.

Critiques of bioethical discourses

The story of bioethics and the current state of ethical guidelines in
medicine is not complete without a consideration of some pointed
criticisms of the principle approach. These criticisms are found
within the principle approach itself, as well as in the emerging
fields of virtue ethics, care ethics, feminist ethics and global ethics.
These critiques share the view that an alternative methodology for
solving moral dilemmas in medicine is forthcoming. Let us consider some of these criticisms, which are by no means exhaustive.
But our discussion will not end here. We also consider criticisms of
the criticisms in order to make the point that in many ways has
already been made – that reducing a discourse, in this case bioethical discourse, to any one system of thought is epistemically and
axiologically problematic and, therefore, bound for failure.

The principle approach has fuelled extensive debates from those
working within its tradition. The debates often concern the relation between and among the principles, particularly in dilemmas
that arise in the medical setting. There are a host of defences for
why autonomy should always override welfare concerns (e.g.
Engelhardt 1996), justice should override autonomy (e.g. Veatch
1986) or sanctity of life should override appeals to autonomy (e.g.
Focus on the Family 2006). For Engelhardt, authority or respect for
person is the linchpin of the moral community. Without respect
for person, there is no morality, including one in medicine. As a
consequence, the principle of autonomy – as a process and not one
filled with content or specific rules – is the necessary condition of
the possibility of a moral situation. This means that any constraint
of autonomy can be considered immoral. For Veatch, it is misleading

to present a moral situation in medicine without appeal to macro-allocational concerns. Medicine is a social enterprise and as such involves the distribution of benefits, burdens and rights. As a consequence, a principle of justice is the overarching concern that guides moral reflection in medicine. For a religious voice, such as Focus on the Family, sanctity of life is a moral principle that can never be weighed against any other (e.g. outcome concerns). Medicine as an enterprise involves the care and cure of patients, who are the creation of God. As a consequence, when thinking through moral dilemmas, one should focus on the sanctity or divine dignity of life, a notion that is rooted in the Abrahamic religious traditions. No doubt, bioethics is alive and well with those articulating and defending their positions.

Then there are criticisms of the principle approach itself. The dominant ones to come on the scene in the past twenty-five years are virtue ethics, care ethics, feminist ethics and global ethics. Virtue ethics dates back to the ancient Greeks and especially Aristotle, who thought that the ethical life is rooted in a person's character as opposed to simply his or her actions. Right action flows out of one's character and a virtuous person has the disposition to see the good. Rules need not be consulted, calculations need not be performed and abstracted duties need not be considered. Upbringing, education, the example of others, reflection, personal effort and experience all play key roles in moral development. In the early twenty-first century, and against the emphasis on autonomy or rights talk, virtue ethics may be seen to serve an important role in bioethics in drawing out discussions of professional and personal character in the health care setting. Stories are written about and by clinicians and patients that highlight the challenges and successes of behaving in certain ways in health care (Clouser & Gert 1990).

Care ethics came on the scene in bioethics in the early 1980s and focuses our attention on the psychological aspects of moral decision-making. Psychologist Carol Gilligan (1982) questioned Laurence Kohlberg's (1971) earlier studies that concluded that women are "less developed" in their moral reasoning skills than men because they do not apply moral principles as universally as men do. Men, Kohlberg reports, tend to focus on a moral dilemma with the aim of deciding which abstract rule applies that may solve the case (e.g. always honour rights). In her studies, Gilligan found that when women are presented with cases of moral conflicts, they focus on the details of the people involved in the situation and their personal relationships. In attempting to resolve the dilemma, women look for compromises and points of agreement, are flexible in their demands and often take novel approaches to find resolutions. In the case of medicine, care ethics rejects the view that abstract principles can capture that which is relevant in making moral decisions. Given that medicine has traditionally been committed to caring for patients, a focus on care and how different decisions affect the relations of the parties involved is seen to be a natural fit.

Feminist ethics rejects the traditional notion that ethics can be represented by a set of abstract principles and that the morality of actions and policies can be assessed by reference to them. For feminists, ethics is part of an ongoing effort to uncover and eliminate sources of social inequality or oppression. Part of rooting out the sources is looking at the nature of ethics itself. For feminists, ethics is in many ways itself a product of the privileged male's domination over women. Any emphasis on rights, for instance, shows preference towards men – who were rights holders and property owners well before women. Because of the importance placed on social inequality, feminists such as Annette Baier (1992) and Susan Sherwin (1992) are concerned with the ways medicine as a social institution tends to subordinate women to men. The predominance of women as nurses, the medicalization of women's conditions such as pregnancy and menopause, and the difference in pay between family practitioners (who care for women and children) and surgeons all point towards areas in medicine needing attention. Although feminist bioethicists certainly cannot be represented as unified in their beliefs and approaches, it is safe to say that they join together in being concerned about unequal or oppressive power relations in the medical setting.

Global ethics increased in popularity with the rise of feminism and 9/11. Feminists began to realize that many did not speak for women of colour, those of diverse socioeconomic status and those who may happily live in cultures other than middle-class capitalist ones. Post 9/11, it becomes increasingly difficult to think simply in terms of national borders and there is the humbling recognition that not all cultures aspire to liberal democratic communities in the same way, if at all. The concerns among global ethicists are the exclusivity of the values in bioethical discourse. Although the popular ethical principles of autonomy, nonmaleficence, beneficence and justice have long-standing historical roots in western philosophy, they derive from and are relevant to liberal, individualistic societies and less to more communitarian ones. South African Keymanthri Moodley (2002) expresses concern about western practices in clinical trials in Africa. Notions such as informed consent will have different meaning and less value in more communitarian cultures. In response to these concerns, Tong (2001) along with others calls for a global account of bioethics, which focuses on shared human conditions such as carnality and mortality. The message is that one needs to be cognizant of the cultural assumptions in the kinds and nature of the values employed in bioethical discourse.

Although the critiques forwarded by those who offer an alternative principle-based approach and an ethics of virtues, care, feminist standpoint or global order have the advantage of leading us to rethink our assumptions in bioethics regarding the values we employ, they assume that all our quandaries will be resolvable once we get hold of another ethical framework, which can then be applied in the way the others that we have rejected have been. In other words, any move to a so-called alternative principled, virtue, care, feminist or global perspective may simply replace one rigid system of thought with another. As we have seen from our prior analysis, this is a problem because any move to a replacement requires a higher-order argument to justify why one system of thought is superior to the other, and ad infinitum. As we have seen in prior chapters, this move is problematic because philosophy and its sub-speciality cannot grant 100 per cent certainty, epistemologically or axiologically.

No doubt, the approaches that have been developed in bio-ethical discourse have made theoretical and practical differences in so far as they have promoted shared and divergent concerns about how medicine is framed and practised. Some have been better at resolving conflict in an efficient manner (e.g. the principles approaches), while others have had the advantage of leading us to pause and appreciate hidden ideological commitments before proceeding (care ethics, feminist ethics and global ethics). Some have promoted robust unification (e.g. the principle approaches), while others have resisted offering it (e.g. certain feminist ethics).

Few have stated what is being stated here: that any account of bioethics that sets itself forth as the definitive methodology to use in the health care setting is suspect. It is suspicious because it advocates what it criticizes, namely the dominance of one system over another. In the end, then, it is self-defeating. It is suspicious because it promises something that medical epistemology and bioethics cannot deliver – that is, easy, concise, definitive answers. As we have shown, this is not forthcoming. It is suspicious because it fails to take into account the dynamic or historical character of medical knowledge and evaluation. The moment an approach is declared "the one" is the moment it ceases to evolve sociohistorically.

Thus we offer what may be called "integrative bioethics", which is our way of talking about discourses of bioethics that are epistemological and axiologically heterogeneous and useful. The lesson is to see such discourses as evolving and relational bodies of knowledge and values set within particular historical, cultural contexts. In this way the feedback loops discussed in Chapter 3 involving the diagnostic, therapeutic and prognostic endeavours in medicine take into consideration bioethical concerns. The resulting loops will be seen to be theoretically and/or practically fruitful in so far as they connect with the lives of those who practise medicine, those who seek the attention of health care professionals and those who administer and oversee medicine. They will in the end be multifaceted, diverse and dynamic as they take into consideration the complexity of the human condition. They will in the end be critical in so far as they allow us to step back and reflect on what concerns us.

Case study reflections

Our conclusion should not come as a surprise. There are choices to be made among alternative epistemologies and ethical accounts of clinical phenomena. Since these choices are not simply determined on traditional rational or theoretical grounds, they will involve a host of considerations involving practical, evaluative, social, cultural, economic and political considerations. The choices framing clinical reality are, then, matters of communal interest. This recognition underscores our responsibilities as individuals who not only know clinical reality but know it in order to manipulate it, and vice versa.

Integrative bioethics offers a way to think about bioethical cases such that cases are not reducible to a single epistemology or principle that appears to operate. Recall the case of coronary artery disease. Coronary artery disease may be considered a genetic, surgical or lifestyle problem depending on whether one is a geneticist, surgeon or public health official. Treatments will vary from genetic engineering to surgery and to behavioural changes. The ethical issues will vary as well depending on how the problem is framed. Should we genetically engineer the offspring of heart patients? Is it ethically permissible for the insurance company to deny heart surgery to a patient who refuses to change lifestyle patterns? Should we stand by and allow schools across the United States to sell high calorie and low nutrition products in the vending machines while they cut programmes in physical education? With each of these questions comes a range of responses drawn from a range of standpoints depending on the interests of the stakeholders. It does not surprise us that we get advice about our heart from a cardiologist, legal advice from a lawyer, spiritual advice from a religious leader and utilitarian guidance from a utilitarian. The fact that answers are in part determined by the methodology used to explore the question fits with what we already know. It should come as no surprise, then, that there will be diverse methodologies operating in a case that brings together various views.

To illustrate our point, let us consider AIDS (Cutter 2003: Ch. 2). If one is attempting to resolve a debate concerning whether HIV causes AIDS or whether HIV testing should remain confidential, one will have to consider the context in which the discussion occurs. Is one talking about AIDS as conceived in the early 1980s, the late 1980s or the early 2000s? In the early 1980s, AIDS referred to a set of phenomenological characteristics, such as high fever, skin blotches, unintentional weight loss and being (or acting) gay. It is not until the late-1980s that AIDS comes to be understood through an aetiological framework, through the actions of a viral entity called HIV (after significant discussion of what term would be appropriate). Research in the 1990s established that HIV is not a simple entity but one that mutates. It does not act alone, but in concert with certain features of the cell, to penetrate and replicate at astonishing levels. Certain behaviours (e.g. anal, but not oral, sex) are conducive to an increase of HIV infection. And in contexts in which women are seen merely as sexual objects, HIV infections among women rise quickly. In this way, AIDS is understood not simply as an aetiological entity but as a multifactorial one.

Note how the treatment offered to an AIDS patient will turn on how AIDS is defined by physicians, understood by researchers and explained by the media. In the earlier years of AIDS, cold compresses and topical ointments were recommended to calm the fever and soothe skin irritations. In the mid-1980s and early 1990s, the fight began to develop a "magic bullet", a pharmacological agent that prevents HIV from infecting or stops it from replicating. In the early to late 1990s, public health recommendations regarding safe sexual practices and AIDS prevention became commonplace – for men as well as for women. And as we saw earlier in the case of South Africa, some see poverty, and not HIV, as responsible for AIDS, and therefore the infusion of money and the eradication of poverty are warranted. Likewise, alternative interventions, such as herbal remedies and diet supplements, were considered just as effective by some as the "cocktail" of drugs prescribed by others. Treatment recommendations turn out to be linked to how one defines or approaches the infection.

Not only is our understanding of a clinical problem related to its treatment, but bioethical discourse will inevitably reflect how we frame the clinical problem. If one understands the clinical problem to be a constellation of signs and symptoms, then much attention will be paid to stereotypes and forms of discrimination that emerge as a response to the clinical problem. We saw this in the early years of the AIDS epidemic with regard to the gay community. Alternatively, if one understands the clinical problem in terms of an aetiological one, a fair amount of focus will be on how to change or prevent the aetiology. Recall the discussions in the 1980s regarding quarantining AIDS patients and mandatory testing for AIDS patients. Then again, if one understands the clinical problem in terms of multifactorial ones, there may be a host of additional issues that enter the discussion. One might look not only at the aetiology of the clinical problem but at other factors, such as the personal, social, economic and political climates that frame the bioethical case. One can begin to see why someone might say that poverty causes AIDS (just as one could say this about a host of other infections, where hygiene is a low priority for daily survival).

Any resolution of a bioethical conflict will depend on the methodology one brings to the conflict resolution and the variables one takes into consideration. If one is committed to rights as the linchpin of the moral community, one will seek to ensure that rights are protected regardless of the outcomes (discrimination, autonomy and privacy). One is reminded of the claim found in the bioethical literature of the past fifteen years that it is important to protect the right of AIDS patients because of the heightened vulnerability they have in a culture that discriminates against gays. If one is a utilitarian, one will seek to maximize benefits and minimize harms at all cost. One is reminded of the US state laws developed in the early 1990s that require HIV testing in order to obtain a marriage licence. Here confidentiality was never an issue, because the community's welfare was paramount. If one is an advocate of a particular religious view, one will seek to ensure that that religious view guides conflict resolution. One is reminded of the debates in K-12 school systems (kindergarten to high-school grades systems that are locally controlled through parent–teacher associations and state licensing) regarding what constitutes appropriate sex education in this era of HIV infection. And we could go on with numerous other examples, such as leukaemia and cardiovascular diseases, that illustrate the need to contextualize any bioethical debate in a sophisticated and broad way (what we call integrative bioethics).

Much in addition will depend on whose rights, interests or salvation are at stake, how and why. Is the concern the rights of an AIDS patient or his or her health care provider, lover or community? Is the focus the interests of HIV-infected males or the women and children who are the involuntary recipients of HIV infection in some cases? Is attention given to the biblical condemnation of homosexual behaviour (in Leviticus) or the call to compassion (found in Matthew's Beatitudes)? Disagreement within seemingly similar standpoints is easy to find, so that, once again, the choice of a context is itself at stake.

In the end, there may not be a resolution to a bioethical conflict in the sense that the resolution is undoubtedly or indisputably true or right. There might be numerous and competing resolutions. And if resources permit, it might be possible to attempt multiple resolutions simultaneously. When resources are scarce, which they often are, compromise will be the only option short of using force to resolve a conflict. But the compromise itself is bound to be challenged, and when it fails, another one may surface as an alternative. In a sense, every compromised solution is an invitation to find another one, so that there is a process of reconfiguration of options as more data are available.

Framing things in this way will involve two skills. A first will be to admit when one does not know. As we have already addressed, uncertainty will be inevitable in bioethical controversy because medicine is a dynamic, evolving enterprise that is both scientific and practical. The challenge will be to come to terms with the uncertainties operating in a case and the trade-offs that will be inevitable, while still having to make a choice. Our inherent ignorance, our human fallibility, should become a battle cry for additional responsibility. It is because we are humbled by the uncertainties of medicine, as physicians and as patients, that we insist on responsible behaviour throughout the process of diagnosis to treatment. Every researcher must remember to limit claims of certainty. Every physician should phrase all clinical diagnoses and prognoses personally and modestly. And every patient should maintain his or her autonomy as an active participant in the process, so that at the end he or she is ultimately responsible for his or her choices. In short, our approach does not support the presumed expertise of the bioethicist as the arbiter of the efficacy or moral character of clinical decisions in a situation.

A second skill will be to admit that a quick answer might not be forthcoming. Framing knowledge claims in terms of what we know and what we do not know, and more often in terms of less than rigorous probability values, takes great knowledge, time, patience and humility. Surely, some would claim that this is not good enough, that a choice must be made right here and now, as in the case of breast implants that were leaking and threatening the lives of thousands of women. Should the courts wait? If yes, for how long? If not, are they stopping potential new data that might prove their decision to have been wrong? In the real world, as some would say, decisions must be quick. But in our view, the pressure to be quick should not jettison the need to deliberate and consider as many variables as possible. One can also interject a caveat along the way, so that critical scrutiny can accompany any decision and allow for changes. Once again, we remain responsible along the way for good and bad choices we have made, and are therefore open to admit to them and make the necessary changes.

Recommendations for practising medicine

Given our analysis of the character of medicine and the state of bioethics, we are drawn to the following conclusions. These conclusions are guides for practice and are themselves open to revision. If we have learned anything from the present study, it is the dynamic character of medical epistemology and of bioethics and the deep sense of uncertainty that permeates the epistemological foundation of medicine. It is because of this and not despite this that we find a renewed urgency in paying attention to our practices, to our interactions among health care providers and patients, and to the level of interpretive engagement and complex reflection that such uncertainty demands (see also Latimer *et al.* 2006). We all must be more rather than less engaged, contribute whatever we find out into the knowledge-loop we alluded to in Chapter 3, and it is in this spirit that we wish to make our proposals or recommendations.

- Unlike television commercials that promise to treat any ailment, we should realize that there are no easy answers in medicine because of the inherent uncertainty and diversity of life. Therefore, do not expect that one prescription will offer you an immediate solution to your medical condition.
- Embrace uncertainty in medicine as an invitation to explore and suggest alternatives, instead of thinking that any equivocation is a sign of ignorance. Therefore, make the effort to consult more than one specialist. When in doubt, keep on searching.
- Appreciate the cultural context of medicine, as opposed to thinking that all medicine is western and scientific. Therefore, bring to bear everything you know from your culture and other cultures when discussing an ailment: you never can tell what factor or variable might be relevant in your case.
- Notice how medical knowledge and medical practice are intimately interrelated. Therefore, pay attention to the process of medical knowing, treating and valuing within socio-historical settings.

- Recognize the ideologies implicit in medical practice, as opposed to thinking that everything is simply scientific. Therefore, examine the deep beliefs of health care providers and the political and legal frameworks they endorse, from the sanctity of human life to the competitive nature of individual existence.

- Approach bioethical controversies carefully: the extreme cases that permeate the media are relatively rare; some come about because of cultural and ideological clashes and not necessarily because of medical disputes. Therefore, do not insist on the application of this or that ethical principle or this or that legal right you might assume you deserve to have.

- Remember that you are simultaneously a patient and a member of society. Therefore, remain a responsible patient and citizen no matter what medical needs you might have at a particular time, and accept the duties associated with your treatment rather than just focusing on your rights.

- Acknowledge that the scientific and medical enterprises are communal and not personal in so far as they require public and private funding. Therefore, do not have false expectations about what can and will be accomplished in medical research and health care provision without public debate (including tax incentives and pecuniary penalties).

- Be modest about your expectations of the perfection of human knowledge. Therefore, do not expect health care providers to perform miracles whenever you need them: they are bound to err and to be incapable of treating your ailment or satisfying your expectations.

- Finally, consider yourself an active participant in the medical enterprise, whether you happen to be a patient, health care provider or healthy citizen. Your life experiences and those of your family and friends are important ingredients and contributing factors that can help us all gain more knowledge of our life and its prospects.

Bibliography

Achenstein, P. 1983. *The Nature of Explanation*. New York: Oxford University Press.

Agassi, J. 1963. *Towards An Historiography of Science*. Middletown, CT: Wesleyan University Press.

Alcoff, L. 1995. "Cultural Feminism versus Post-Structuralism: The Identity Crisis in Feminist Theory". In *Feminism and Philosophy: Essential Readings*, N. Tuana & R. Tong (eds), 434–56. Boulder, CO: Westview.

Amundsen, D. 1977. "The Liability of the Physician in Classical Greek Legal Theory and Practice". *Journal of the History of Medicine and Allied Sciences* **32** (April): 172–203.

Amundsen, D. 1981. "Casuistry and Professional Obligations: The Regulations of Physicians by the Court of Conscience in the Late Middle Ages" (Part 1). *Transactions and Studies of the College of Physicians of Philadelphia* **3**: 22–39.

Annas, G. J. 1988. *Judging Medicine*. Totowa, NJ: Humana Press.

Annas, G. J. & S. Elias (eds) 1992. *Gene Mapping: Using Law and Ethics as Guides*. Oxford: Oxford University Press.

Annas, G. J. & M. A. Grodin (eds) 1992. *The Nazi Doctors and the Nuremberg Code: Human Rights in Human Experimentation*. Oxford: Oxford University Press.

Annis, D. 1978. "A Contextual Theory of Epistemic Justification". *American Philosophical Quarterly* **15**: 213–19.

Antony, L. 2002. "Quine as Feminist: The Radical Import of Naturalized Epistemology". In *A Mind of One's Own*, 2nd edn, L. M. Antony & C. E. Witt (eds), 110–53. Boulder, CO: Westview.

Aristotle 1985. *Nicomachean Ethics*, T. Irwin (trans.). Indianapolis, IN: Hackett.

Augustine 1999. *Confessions of Saint Augustine*. Washington, DC: Logos Research Systems, Inc.

Avery, O. T. *et al.* 1944. "Studies on the Chemical Nature of the Substance Inducing Transformation of Pneumococcal Types. Induction of Transformation by a Deoxyribonucleic Acid Function Isolate from Pneumococcal Type III". *Journal of Experimental Medicine* **79**: 137–58.

Ayer, A. J. 1952. *Language, Truth and Logic*. New York: Dover (first published 1936).

Ayer, A. J. (ed.) 1959. *Logical Positivism*. New York: The Free Press.

Bacon, F. 1985. *The New Organon*. New York: Macmillan (first published 1620).

Baier, A. 1992. "Alternative Offerings to Asclepius". *Medical Humanities Review* **6**(1): 9–19.

Bates, D. (ed.) 1995. *Knowledge and the Scholarly Medical Traditions*. Cambridge: Cambridge University Press.

Beauchamp, T. L. & J. F. Childress 2001. *Principles of Biomedical Ethics*, 5th edn. New York: Oxford University Press.

Bender, F. L. 2003. *The Culture of Extinction: Toward a Philosophy of Deep Ecology*. New York: Humanity Books.

Bentham, J. 1970. *An Introduction to the Principles of Morals and Legislation*. Darien, CT: Hafner Publishing (first published 1789).

Bichat, X. 1981. "Pathological Anatomy: Preliminary Discourse". In *Concepts of Health and Disease: Interdisciplinary Perspectives*, A. L. Caplan *et al.* (eds), 167–73. Boston, MA: Addison-Wesley (first published 1827).

Brody, B. A. & N. Capaldi (eds) 1968. *Science: Men, Methods, Goals*. New York and Amsterdam: W. A. Benjamin.

Boerhaave, H. 1742–6. *Institutes, Dr. Boerhaave's Academical Lectures on the Theory of Physics* [6 vols]. London: W. Innys (first published 1708).

Chisholm, R. 2003. "Contemporary Classical Foundationalism". In *The Theory of Knowledge*, L. P. Pojman (ed.), 163–82. Belmont, CA: Wadsworth (first published 1977).

Chopra, D. 2003. *The Spontaneous Fulfillment of Desire: Harnessing the Infinite Power of Coincidence*. New York: Harmony.

Clouser, K. D. & B. Gert 1990. "A Critique of Principalism". *Journal of Medicine and Philosophy* 15(2): 219–36.

Clouser, K. D. & D. J. Hufford 1993. "Nonorthodox Medical Systems: Their Epistemological Claims". *Journal of Medicine and Philosophy* 18(2): 101–31.

Code of Federal Regulations, Protection of Human Subjects 2005. "45 CFR Part 46", http://ohsr.od.nih.gov/guidelines/45cfr46.html [accessed 3 August 2005].

Cohen, I. B. 1985. *Revolution in Science*. Cambridge, MA: Harvard University Press.

Colton, I. B. 1974. *Statistics in Medicine*. Boston: Little Brown.

Comte, A. 1975. *Auguste Comte and Positivism: The Essential Writings*, G. Lenzer (ed.). New York: Harper & Row.

Comte, A. 1988. *Introduction to Positive Philosophy*, F. Ferre (trans. & ed.). Indianapolis, IN: Hackett (first published 1829).

Condorcet, A. de 1979. *Sketch for a Historical Picture of the Progress of the Human Mind*, J. Barraclough (trans.). Westport, CT: Greenwood (first published 1795).

Cowley, G. & K. Springen 2002. "The End of the Age of Estrogen?" *Newsweek* (22 July): 38–41.

Cullen, W. 1769. *Synopsis nosologiae methodicae*. Edinburgh: William Creech.

Cutter, M. A. G. 1992. "Value Presuppositions in Diagnosis: A Case Study of Cervical Cancer". In *The Ethics of Diagnosis*, J. Peset (ed.), 147–54. Amsterdam: Kluwer.

Cutter, M. A. G. 1997. "Engelhardt's Analysis of Disease: Implications for a Feminist Epistemology". In *Reading Engelhardt*, B. Minogue *et al.* (eds), 139–48. Amsterdam: Kluwer.

Cutter, M. A. G. 2002a. "Local Bioethics Discourse: In Search of Grounding". In *Cross-Cultural Perspectives on the (Im)possibility of Global Bioethics*, J. Po-wah (ed.), 319–34. Amsterdam: Kluwer.

Cutter, M. A. G. 2002b. "The Mind's Eye and the Hand's Brain: On Wartofsky's Philosophy of Medicine". In *Constructivism and Practice: Toward a Social and Historical Epistemology*, C. Gould (ed.), 243–57. New York: Rowman & Littlefield.

Cutter, M. A. G. 2003. *Reframing Disease Contextually*. Amsterdam: Kluwer.

Cutter, M. A. G. 2005. "Expert Moral Choice in Medicine: A Study of Certainty and Locality". In *Ethics Expertise: History, Contemporary Perspectives, and Applications*, L. Rasmussen (ed.), 125–37. Amsterdam: Springer.

Cutter, M. A. G. & E. E. Shelp (eds) 1991. *Competency: A Study of Informal Competency Determinations in Primary Care*. Amsterdam: Kluwer.

Dancy, J. 1985. "A Defense of Coherentism". In *The Theory of Knowledge*, L. P. Pojman (ed.), 206–15. Belmont, CA: Wadsworth.

Delkeskamp-Hayes, C. & M. A. G. Cutter (eds) 1993. *Science, Technology, and the Art of Medicine: European-American Dialogues*. Amsterdam: Kluwer.

DeRose, K. 1992. "Contextualism and Knowledge Attribution". *Philosophy and Phenomenological Research* **52**: 913–29.

Descartes, R. 1980. *Discourse on Method* and *Meditations on First Philosophy*. Indianapolis, IN: Hackett (first published 1637 and 1641, respectively).

Dewey, J. 1960. *The Quest for Certainty: A Study of the Relation of Knowledge and Action*. New York: Capricorn Books.

Duesberg, P. H. 1988. "HIV is Not the Cause of AIDS". *Science* **241**: 514–17.

Engel, G. 1977. "The Need for a New Medical Model: A Challenge for Biomedicine". *Science* **196**: 129–36.

Engelhardt, H. T. Jr 1981. "Disease of Masturbation". In *Concepts of Health and Disease: Interdisciplinary Perspectives*, A. L. Caplan *et al.* (eds), 267–80. Boston, MA: Addison-Wesley (first published 1974).

Engelhardt, H. T. Jr 1996. *The Foundations of Bioethics*. New York: Oxford University Press.

Feinstein, A. 1967. *Clinical Judgment*. Baltimore, MD: Williams and Wilkins.

Feyerabend, P. 1975. *Against Method: Outline of an Anarchistic Theory of Knowledge*. London: Verso.

Fleck, L. 1979. *Genesis and Development of a Scientific Fact*. F. Bradley & T. J. Trenn (trans.), T. J. Trenn & R. K. Merton (eds). Chicago, IL: University of Chicago Press (first published 1935).

Fletcher, J. 1960. *Morals and Medicine*. Boston, MA: Beacon Press (first published 1954).

Focus on the Family 2006. "Sanctity of Life: A Foundation of the Christian Life". *Christian Worldview* (22 August), http://www.family.org

Foucault, M. 1973. *The Birth of the Clinic: An Archeology of Medical Perception*, A. M. Sheridan Smith (trans.). New York: Pantheon (first published 1963).

Galen 1985. *Three Treatises on the Nature of Science*, R. Walzer & M. Frede (trans.). Indianapolis, IN: Hackett.

Galilei, Galileo 1953. *Dialogue Concerning the Two Chief Worlds*, S. Drake (trans.). Berkeley, CA: University of California Press (first published 1632).

Garrison, F. 1929. *An Introduction to the History of Medicine.* Philadelphia, PA: Saunders.

Gawande, A. 2007. *Better: A Surgeon's Note on Performance.* New York: Metropolitan Books.

Gellner, E. 1979. *Legitimization of Belief.* Cambridge: Cambridge University Press.

Gifford, N. L. 1983. *An Introduction to Relativism and Knowledge.* New York: SUNY Press.

Gilligan, C. 1982. *In A Different Voice.* Cambridge, MA: Harvard University Press.

Gillispie, C. C. 1960. *The Edge of Objectivity: An Essay in the History of Scientific Ideas.* Princeton, NJ: Princeton University Press.

Glossary of Culture Bound Syndromes 2006. http://www.weber.ucsd. edu/thall/cbs [accessed 4 August 2006].

Goldstein, R. 2005. *Incompleteness: The Proof and Paradox of Kurt Gödel.* New York: Norton.

Gorovitz, S. 1982. *Doctors' Dilemmas: Moral Conflict and Medical Care.* New York: Macmillan.

Gorovitz, S. 1985. "Ethical Dilemmas in Medicine: Easy Ones, Hard Ones, and the Difference Between Them". Unpublished paper, Medical Ethics Grand Rounds, Boston University School of Medicine, 5 November.

Gorovitz, S. & A. MacIntyre 1976. "Toward a Theory of Medical Fallibility". *Journal of Medicine and Philosophy* 1: 51–71.

Groopman, J. 2006. "The Preeclampsia Puzzle: Making Sense of a Mysterious Pregnancy Disorder". *The New Yorker* (July 24): 26–32.

Groopman, J. 2007. *How Doctors Think?* New York: Houghton Mifflin.

Hanson, N. R. 1958. *Patterns of Discovery: An Inquiry into the Conceptual Foundation of Science.* Cambridge: Cambridge University Press.

Hanson, N. R. 1971. *Observation and Exploration: A Guide to Philosophy of Science.* New York: Harper & Row.

Haraway, D. 1991. *Simians, Cyborgs, and Women: The Reinvention of Nature.* New York: Routledge.

Harvey, A. M., R. J. Johns, A. H. Owens & R. S. Ross 1972. *The Principles and Practice of Medicine*. New York: Appleton Century Crofts.

Helsinki Declaration 1964. The Online Ethics Center for Engineering and Science, Case Western Reserve University, http://onlineethics. org/reseth/helsinki.html [accessed 4 August 2006].

Hempel, C. G. 1965. *Aspects of Scientific Explorations*. New York: The Free Press.

Henig, R. M. 2006. "Fat Factors". *The New York Times Magazine* (13 August): 28–33.

Hesse, M. 1966. *Models and Analogies in Science*. Notre Dame, IN: University of Notre Dame Press.

Hippocrates 1943. *Regimen*, W. H. S. Jones (trans.). Cambridge, MA: Harvard University Press.

Holton, G. 2005. *Victory and Vexation in Science: Einstein, Bohr, Heisenberg, and Others*. Cambridge, MA: Harvard University Press.

Hudson, R. P. 1983. *Disease and Its Control: The Shaping of Modern Thought*. Westport, CT: Greenwood.

Hume, D. 1978. *A Treatise of Human Nature*, L. A. Selby-Bigge (ed.). Oxford: Oxford University Press (first published 1740).

Illingworth, P. & W. E. Parmet 2006. *Ethical Health Care*. Englewood Cliffs, NJ: Prentice Hall.

Johanssen, W. 1909. *Elemente der exacten Erblichkeitslehre*. Jena: Gustar Fischer.

Jonsen, A. R. 1998. *The Birth of Bioethics*. New York: Oxford University Press.

Jones, J. 1981. *Bad Blood*. New York: The Free Press.

Juengst, E. T. 1995. "The Ethics of Prediction: Genetic Risk and the Physician–Patient Relationship". *Genome Science and Technology* 1(1): 21–36.

Juengst, E. T. 1998. "Caught in the Middle Again: Professional Ethical Considerations in Genetic Testing for Health Risks". *Genetic Testing* 1(3): 189–200.

Kant, I. 1970. "An Answer to the Question: What is Enlightenment?" In *Kant's Political Writings*, H. B. Nisbet (trans.) & H. Reiss (ed.), 41–48. Cambridge: Cambridge University Press (first published 1784).

Kant, I. 1985. *Foundations of the Metaphysic of Morals*. New York: Macmillan (first published 1785).

Kant, I. 1987. *Critique of Pure Reason*, N. K. Smith (trans.). New York: St Martin's Press (first published 1789).

Katz, J. 1984a. *The Silent World of Doctor and Patient*. New York: The Free Press.

Katz, J. 1984b. "Why Doctors Don't Disclose Uncertainty". *The Hastings Center Report* **10**: 35–44.

Khushf, G. 1999. "The Aesthetics of Clinical Judgment: Exploring the Link Between Diagnostic Elegance and Effective Resource Utilization". *Medicine, Health Care, and Philosophy* 2: 141–59.

King, L. S. 1982. *Medical Thinking: A Historical Preface*. Princeton, NJ: Princeton University Press.

Koch, R. 1932. *The Aetiology of Tuberculosis*. New York: National Tuberculosis Association (first published 1882).

Kohlberg, L. 1971. *The Philosophy of Moral Development*. New York: Harper & Row.

Konold, D. N. 1978. "Codes of Medical Ethics: History". In *Encyclopedia of Bioethics*, W. T. Reich (ed.), 162–71. New York: The Free Press.

Kuhn, T. S. 1970. *The Structure of Scientific Revolutions*, 2nd edn. Chicago, IL: University of Chicago Press.

Laënnec, T. 1834. *Treatise on Medical Ausculation and the Diseases of the Lungs and Heart*. London.

Laín-Entralgo, P. 1970. *Therapies of the World in Classical Antiquity*. New Haven, CT: Yale University Press.

Lander, E. S. & N. J. Schrok 1994. "Genetic Dissection of Complex Traits". *Science* **265**: 2037–48.

Latimer, J., K. Featherstone, P. Atkinson, A. Clarke, D. T. Pilz & A. Shaw 2006. "Rebirthing the Clinic: The Interaction of Clinical Judgment and Genetic Technology in the Production of Medical Science". *Science, Technology, and Human Values* **31**(5): 599–630.

Latour, B. 1987. *Science in Action: How to Follow Scientists and Engineers through Society*. Cambridge, MA: Harvard University Press.

Latour, B. 1988. *The Pasteurization of France*, A. Sheridan & J. Law (trans.). Cambridge, MA: Harvard University Press.

Latour, B. 1990. "Postmodern? No, Simply Amodern! Steps toward an Anthropology of Science". *Studies in the History and Philosophy of Science* **21**: 145–71.

Latour, B. & S. Woolgar 1986. *Laboratory Life: The Construction of Scientific Facts*. Princeton, NJ: Princeton University Press.

Le Fanu, J. 2000. *The Rise and Fall of Modern Medicine*. New York: Carroll & Graf.

Lewontin, R. C. 1993. *Biology as Ideology: The Doctrine of DNA*. New York: HarperCollins.

Lloyd, G. E. R. 1995. "Epistemological Arguments in Early Greek Medicine in Comparativist Perspective". In *Knowledge and the Scholarly Medical Traditions*, D. Bates (ed.), 25–40. Cambridge: Cambridge University Press.

Longino, H. 1990. *Science as a Social Knowledge: Values, and Objectivity in Scientific Inquiry*. Princeton, NJ: Princeton University Press.

Longino, H. 1997. "Feminist Epistemology as a Local Epistemology". *Proceedings of the Aristotelian Society: Supplementary Volume* **71**(1): 19–36.

Lyotard, J.-F. 1984. *The Postmodern Condition: A Report on Knowledge*. Minneapolis, MN: University of Minnesota Press.

McInerney, J. D. & R. Moore 1993. "Voting in Science: Raise Your Hand if You Want Humans to Have 48 Chromosomes". *The American Biology Teacher* **55**(3): 132–3.

Maimonides, M. 2000. *The Guide for the Perplexed*. New York: Dover.

Markon, J. 2006. "Fight Over a Child's Care Ends in Compromise". *Washington Post* (17 August): A1.

Marx, K. 1961. *Economic and Philosophic Manuscripts of 1844*, M. Milligan (trans.). Moscow: Foreign Languages Publishing House.

Mayr, E. 1982. *The Growth of Biological Thought: Diversity, Evolution, and Inheritance*. Cambridge, MA: Harvard University Press.

Mayr, E. 1997. *This Is Biology: The Science of the Living World*. Cambridge, MA: Harvard University Press, 1997.

Mendel, G. 1866. "Versuche über Pflanzenhybriden". *Verhandlungen naturaforschenden Vereins Brünn* **4**: 3–44.

Menzel, P. 1992. "Equality, Autonomy, and Efficiency: What Health Care System Should We Have?" *Journal of Medicine and Philosophy* **17**: 33–57.

Merton, R. K. 1973. *The Sociology of Science: Theoretical and Empirical Investigations*. Chicago, IL: University of Chicago Press.

Mill, J. S. 2002. *Utilitarianism*, 2nd edn, X. Sher (ed.). Indianapolis, IN: Hackett (first published 1861).

Moodley, K. 2002. "HIV Vaccine Trial Participation in South Africa – An Ethical Assessment". *Journal of Medicine and Philosophy* **27**(2): 197–215.

Moore, J. A. 1992. *Science as a Way of Knowing: The Foundation of Modern Biology*. Cambridge, MA: Harvard University Press.

Morgagni, G. B. 1981. "The Author's Preface", *The Seats and Causes of Disease*. In *Concepts of Health and Disease*, A. L. Caplan *et al.* (eds), 157–65. Boston, MA: Addison-Wesley (first published 1761).

Murphy, E. 1976. *The Logic of Medicine*. Baltimore, MD: Johns Hopkins University Press.

National Academy of Sciences 1998. *Teaching About Evolution and the Nature of Science*. Washington, DC: National Academy Press.

National Commission for the Protection of Human Subjects of Biomedical and Behavioral Research 1978. *The Belmont Report*. Washington, DC: DHEW Publication OS 78-0012, http://ohsr.od.hin.gov/guidelines/belmont.html [accessed 30 July 2006].

Nietzsche, F. 1974. *Gay Science*, W. Kaufman (trans.). New York: Vintage (first published 1887).

Northrup, C. 1998. *Women's Bodies, Women's Wisdom*. New York: Bantam.

O'Neill, O. 2002. *Autonomy and Trust in Bioethics*. Cambridge: Cambridge University Press.

Parusnikova, Z. 2002. "Integrative Medicine: Partnership or Control?" *Studies in the History and Philosophy of Biological and Biomedical Sciences* **33**: 169–86.

Pasteur, L. 1942. *Memoirs on the Organic Corpuscles which Exist in the Atmosphere*. In *Source Book of Medical History*, L. Clandenning (ed.) & D. H. Clandenning (trans.). New York: Dover (first published 1862).

Pellegrino, E. D. 1976. "Philosophy of Medicine: Problematic and Potential". *Journal of Medicine and Philosophy* **1**(March): 5–31.

Pellegrino, E. D. & D. Thomasma 1981. *A Philosophical Basis of Medical Practice*. New York: Oxford University Press.

Pence, G. 2000. *Classical Cases in Medical Ethics: Accounts of Cases that Have Shaped Medical Ethics*, 3rd edn. New York: McGraw-Hill.

Percival, T. 1975. *Medical Ethics*. New York: Robert A. Krieger.

Permissible Medical Experiments n.d. *Trials of War Criminals Before the Nuremberg Military Tribunals Under Control Council Law No. 10: Nuremberg, October 1946–April 1949*, vol. 2. Washington, DC: US Government Printing Office.

Plato 1992. *The Republic*, 2nd edn, G. M. A. Grube (trans.), C. D. C. Reeve (rev.). Indianapolis, IN: Hackett.

Po-wah, J. T. L. (ed.) 2002. *Cross-Cultural Perspectives on the (Im)Possibility of Global Bioethics*. Amsterdam: Kluwer.

Ethical Choices in Contemporary Medicine

Polanyi, M. 1966. *The Tacit Dimension*. New York: Doubleday.

Popper, K. R. 1957. *The Poverty of Historicism*. New York: Harper & Row.

Popper, K. R. 1959. *The Logic of Scientific Discovery*. New York: Harper & Row (first published 1935).

Popper, K. R. 1966. *The Open Society and Its Enemies*. Princeton, NJ: Princeton University Press.

Popper, K. R. 1976. *Unended Quest, An Intellectual Autobiography*. Chicago, IL: Open Court.

Portin, P. 2002. "Historical Development of the Concept of the Gene". *Journal of Medicine and Philosophy* **27**(3): 257–86.

Regan, T. & P. Singer 1989. *Animal Rights and Human Obligations*, 2nd edn. Englewood Cliffs, NJ: Prentice Hall.

Roberts, D. 1996. "Women and Medicine". In *Feminism and Bioethics: Beyond Reproduction*, S. Wolf (ed.), 116–43. New York: Oxford University Press.

Rothenberg, P. S. 2001. *Race, Class, and Gender in the United States: An Integrated Study*, 5th edn. New York: Worth.

Rush, B. 1813. *Medical Observations and Inquiries*. Pennsylvania (first published 1789).

Sass, H.-M. 1983. "Reichsrundschreiden 1931: Pre-Nuremberg German Regulations Concerning New Therapy and Human Experimentation". *Journal of Medicine and Philosophy* **8** (May): 99–111.

Sassower, R. 1990a. "Medical Education: The Training of Ethical Physicians". *Studies in Philosophy and Education* **10**: 251–61.

Sassower, R. 1990b. "Scarcity and Setting the Boundaries of Political Economy". *Social Epistemology* **4**(1): 75–91.

Sassower, R. 1995. *Cultural Collisions: Postmodern Technoscience*. New York: Routledge.

Sassower, R. 1997. *Technoscientific Angst: Ethics and Responsibility*. Minneapolis, MN: University of Minnesota Press.

Sassower, R. 2006. *Popper's Legacy: Rethinking Politics, Economics and Science*. Chesham: Acumen.

Sassower, R. & M. Grodin 1986. "Epistemological Questions Concerning Death". *Death Studies* **10**: 341–53.

Sassower, R. & M. Grodin 1988. "Beyond Medical Ethics: New Directions for Philosophy and Medicine". *Journal of Medical Humanities and Bioethics* **9**: 121–34.

Sauvages de Lacroix, F. B. 1768. *Nosologia methodica sistens morborum classes juxta Sydenhami mentem et botanicorum ordinem* [5 vols]. Amsterdam: Fratrum de Tournes.

Sherwin, S. 1992. *No Longer Patient: Feminist Ethics and Health Care*. Philadelphia, PA: Temple University Press.

Shrader-Frechette, K. S. 1980. *Nuclear Power and Public Policy: The Social and Ethical Problems of Fission Technology*. Amsterdam: Reidel.

Sinclair, W. J. 1932. *Semmelweis: His Life and His Doctrine*. Manchester: Manchester University Press (first published 1882).

Specter, M. 2000. "The Pharmageddon Riddle: Did Monsanto Want More Profits, or Did it Want to Save the World?" *The New Yorker* (April 10): 58–71.

Starr, P. 1982. *The Social Transformation of American Medicine*. New York: Basic Books.

Sydenham, T. 1981. "Preface to the Third Edition". In *Concepts of Health and Disease: Interdisciplinary Perspectives*, A. L. Caplan *et al.* (eds), 145–55. Boston, MA: Addison-Wesley.

Szasz, T. 1961. *Myth of Mental Illness*. New York: Harper-Hoeber.

Talbot, M. 2000. "The Placebo Prescription". *The New York Times Magazine* (January 9): 34–9, 44, 58–60.

Tauber, A. I. 2005. *Patient Autonomy and the Ethics of Responsibility*. Cambridge, MA: MIT Press.

Todhunter, I. 1865. *A History of the Mathematical Theory of Probability, From the Time of Pascal to that of Laplace*. Cambridge: Macmillan.

Tong, R. 2001. "Toward a Feminist Bioethics: Addressing Women's Health Concerns Worldwide". *Health Care Analysis* **9**: 229–46.

Tong, R., with G. Anderson & A. Santos 2000. *Globalizing Feminist Bioethics: Cross-Cultural Perspectives*. Boulder, CO: Westview.

Toulmin, S. 1961. *Foresight and Understanding: An Inquiry into the Aims of Science*. New York: Harper & Row.

Tuana, N. 1988. "The Weaker Seed: The Sexist Bias of Reproductive Theory" *Hypatia* **3**(1): 35–59.

Urmson, J. O. 1956. *Philosophical Analysis: Its Development Between the Two World Wars*. Oxford: Oxford University Press.

Varmus, H. 1989. "Naming the Aids Virus". In *Meaning of AIDS: Perspectives From the Humanities*, E. T. Juengst & B. A. Koenig (eds), 3–11. New York: Praeger.

Ethical Choices in Contemporary Medicine

Veatch, R. M. 1986. *The Foundation of Justice: Why the Retarded and the Rest of Us Have Claims to Equality*. New York: Oxford University Press.

Virchow, R. 1981. "One Hundred Years of General Pathology". In *Concepts of Health and Disease: Interdisciplinary Perspectives*, A. L. Caplan *et al.* (eds), 190–95. Boston, MA: Addison-Wesley (first published 1895).

Wartofsky, M. 1976. "The Mind's Eye and the Hand's Brain: Toward an Historical Epistemology of Medicine". In *Science, Ethics, and Medicine*, H. T. Engelhardt Jr. & D. Callahan (eds), 167–94. New York: The Hastings Center.

Wartofsky, M. 1992. "The Social Presuppositions of Medical Knowledge". In *The Ethics of Diagnosis*, J. I. Peset & D. Garcia (eds), 131–51. Amsterdam: Kluwer.

Watson, J. D. & F. H. Crick 1953. "Molecular Structure of Nucleic Acids". *Nature* **171**: 737.

Wear, A. 1995. "Epistemology and Learned Medicine in Early Modern England". In *Knowledge and the Scholarly Medical Traditions*, D. Bates (ed.), 151–73. Cambridge: Cambridge University Press.

Weber, M. 1978. *Economy and Society: An Outline of Interpretive Sociology*, G. Roth & C. Wittiek (eds). Berkeley, CA: University of California Press.

Weil, A. T. 2004. *Natural Health, Natural Medicine: The Complete Guide to Wellness and Self-Care for Optimum Health*. New York: Houghton Mifflin.

World Health Association 2003. "Nutrition, Health, and Human Rights". *World Health Association*, http://www.who.int/nut/nutrition.htm [accessed 8 June 2006].

Wulff, H. R. 1981. *Rational Diagnosis and Treatment: An Introduction to Clinical Decision-Making*. Oxford: Blackwell.

Wulff, H. R. 1986. *Philosophy of Medicine: An Introduction*. Oxford: Blackwell.

Yoxen, E. 1983. *The Gene Business: Who Should Control Biotechnology?* New York: Harper & Row.

Index